Inside the Norton AntiVirus

by
Peter Norton
and
Paul Nielsen

Brady Publishing

New York　　London　　Toronto　　Sydney　　Tokyo　　Singapore

Brady Publishing

A Division of Prentice Hall Computer Publishing
15 Columbus Circle
New York, NY 10023

Manufactured in the United States of America

10 9 8 7 6 5 4 3 2 1

ISBN: 0-13-473463-7

For Melissa, the beauty in my life.

Acknowledgments

A book about such a dynamic topic as computer viruses requires the knowledge and assistance of several individuals. I'd like to thank each of you for your contribution:

Thanks to Peter Norton for writing *Inside the IBM PC*, the first PC book I purchased ten years ago, and for making this book possible.

Richard Sekar, Nathan Ginosar, Mohan Gopalakrishnan, Cory Haibloom, Bob Kirkland, David Shannon, and the entire Norton AntiVirus team of Symantec/Peter Norton Computing Group, for developing an excellent product and patiently answering all my questions.

Bill Gladstone and Matt Wagner of Waterside Productions

Kevin Goldstein and Scott Clark, of Peter Norton Books, for making this project possible.

Dave C. Johnson, for your hours of editing and your many suggestions.

Patricia Hoffman, the antivirus industry's virus librarian, for your expertise, assistance, and for your efforts to bring order to chaos.

Rose Kearsley, of Novell, for providing suggestions and technical information.

Rick Roth, of Artisoft, for lending technical insights.

Thanks to the other virus fighters who contributed their thoughts and suggestions: Jim Jester, David Hefner, Gary Lail, Troy Helms, and Rob Potter.

Limits of Liability and Disclaimer of Warranty

The authors and publisher of this book have put forth their best efforts in preparing this book and the programs contained in it. These efforts include the development, research, and testing of the theories and programs to determine their effectiveness. The authors and publisher make no warranty of any kind, expressed or implied, with regard to these programs or the documentation contained in this book. The authors and publisher shall not be liable in any event for incidental or consequential damages in connection with, or arising out of, the furnishing, performance, or use of these programs.

Trademarks

Most computer and software brand names have trademarks or registered trademarks. The individual trademarks have not been listed here.

Credits

Publisher
Michael Violano

Managing Editor
Kelly D. Dobbs

Editor
Tracy Smith

Production Editors
Tom Dillon
Jill D. Bond

Book Designer
Scott Cook

Cover Designer
HUB Graphics

Production Team
Christine Cook
Joelynn Gifford
Denny Hager
Carla Hall-Batton
John Kane
Roger Morgan
Michelle Self
Greg Simsic
Angie Trzepacz

Contents

Introduction

Why Read this Book?

Whether you are a consultant specializing in LAN security, a user interested in virus-free computing, or a user tasked with corporate-level PC support, you'll find this book to be an interesting guide to rogue software, safe computing, and using Norton AntiVirus.

Each chapter has been written so that you can read any one chapter and it will explain what you need to know.

Section 1: Rogue Software

The culture, weapons, and methods of computer terrorism, as well as the specifics of computer viruses, are covered in this broad overview of rogue software. Rogue software is clouded in myth; this section tries to replace some of the rumors with facts.

This section offers strategies and tactics for watching for and fighting viruses. Safe computing guidelines and the theories behind them are also included in a straightforward format.

Section 2: Using Norton AntiVirus

Here you'll find the detailed information you need to set up and use Virus Intercept and Virus Clinic. Specific information is presented in depth concerning removing viruses.

Section 3: Advanced Norton AntiVirus

Keeping your copy of Norton AntiVirus current with the NAV Virus Identification Lab means that you have the best protection possible against new viruses. Chapter 7 covers the many ways to receive new virus signatures and update Norton AntiVirus.

Norton Desktop for Windows is a highly acclaimed bestseller, and Norton AntiVirus works seamlessly under Windows as well as under DOS. We'll talk about Windows-specific concepts here.

A virus on a LAN can spread incredibly fast. This section contains strategies and tips for disinfecting a LAN and keeping the LAN virus-free. Novell Netware and LANtastic each offer built-in security that goes beyond the security of a single-user MS-DOS system. Tips on how to use the network's security for a smooth-running virus-free LAN are also included.

If You Suspect a Virus Now...

If you suspect a virus may have infected your computer and you don't have time to read this entire book, here are the quick and dirty steps to removing a virus. No theory or explanation, just the facts:

"Don't Panic"

1. Rule number one when facing any crisis—**Remain Calm**. Panicking will only cause your logic to become befuddled. Chances are that the virus you have just noticed has been on your computer for a while and you are just now seeing symptoms.

2. Chances are that you already use Norton AntiVirus, but if you just bought it, don't install it yet. We need to remove the virus before Norton AntiVirus is installed on your hard drive.

3. Physically turn off your computer, don't just warm boot (Ctrl-Alt-Del).

4. Find an original DOS diskette or a known virus-free bootable diskette.

5. Write-protect the diskette and then reboot using the boot diskette.

6. Once the PC is booted, try to view a directory of the C: drive (DIR C: <Enter>). If you get a disk read error or anything but a proper directory, run Norton Disk Doctor and/or Norton Disk Tools (Norton Utilities) to attempt to repair the hard disk. If you previously made a copy of your boot sector and partition table with Norton Rescue (using Norton AntiVirus, Norton Desktop, or Norton Utilities), try to restore the Rescue data.

7. Place the Norton AntiVirus diskette in the drive and run Norton AntiVirus Virus Clinic (NAV <Enter>).

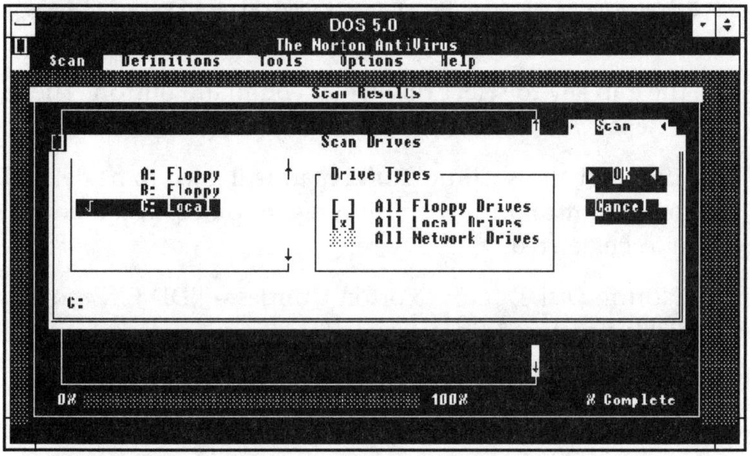

Figure I-1 Virus Clinic defaults to scan All Local Drives

8. Virus Clinic defaults to scan All Local Drives. This is the option you want, so just press Enter to accept the selection and begin the scan.

9. If you do in fact have a virus, Virus Clinic will identify the virus(es) and infected file(s) as they are found on the disk.

10. When the scan is complete, press Tab to select the print command button. Print the results of the scan as a record of the infection.

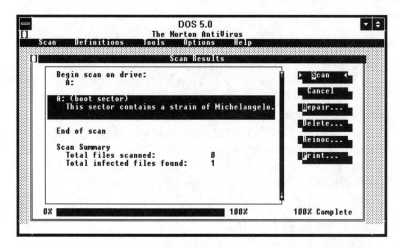

Figure I-2 Having found the virus, Virus Clinic is ready to repair the Boot Sector

11. Use the Tab key to select the Repair command button. Then select Repair All.

12. Any files that Virus Clinic can't repair will need to be deleted. You may want to print the results again to help you identify the file(s) to be deleted.

13. Run Norton Disk Doctor (Norton Utilities—NDD.EXE) to be sure the disk's structure is intact.

Rogue Software

Rogue software is any program that runs on your computer without your knowledge and consent. Rogue software comes in many sizes, colors, and flavors; an ANSI Bomb can reprogram your keyboard so that the F1 key becomes Format C:; a programmer may leave a secret back door in a custom payroll program and later change a salary figure; or, the Jerusalem virus could delete a program.

Any known, intentional threat tends to cause panic alarms and put the media into hyper-alert. Wars have been started because of public fears. Computer viruses and other rogue software are indeed a danger. The best response to that threat is sound information and an understanding of the threat. Only then can you develop and adopt a realistic plan to minimize the possibility of encountering rogue software and prevent any damage.

This section's first chapter presents an overview of the many types of rogue software, their origins, and the myths that surround them.

The second chapter takes a closer look at the various types of viruses and their life cycles along with the anatomy of the three most common viruses: the Stoned, Jerusalem, and Michelangelo viruses. Chapter 2 closes with a discussion of the inherent weaknesses of viruses.

Strategies for Safe Computing is a complete list of tips to help you avoid typical computer problems as well as viruses.

About Rogue Software

Computer viruses have become a fact of life.

A few years ago, the term "computer gremlin" meant a hardware glitch or a software bug. In the early years of computing, hard disks were prone to failure (remember when a hard disk with 0 bad sectors was a rare thing?). Software had few safeguards to protect data. Hardware has since become more reliable and software has also made great strides toward being accident-proof.

Today's problems include finding a flicker-free match between a 1024 by 768 resolution video card and a 16-inch monitor, deciding where to install your new 13Mb word processor, the correct loading order for your eight memory resident programs (TSRs), and configuring your expanded memory regions to hold those eight TSRs while still leaving 621Kb of Base memory available. Today, "upgrading your system" refers to installing a 486 motherboard or adding another 212Mb hard disk. When Brady first published *Inside the IBM PC*, upgrading meant adding a 256Kb memory board or moving up to a Hercules high-resolution graphics video board.

And now we have computer viruses.

Reading though the conversations on the CompuServe Virus Help Forum and other bulletin boards, one recurring theme is prevalent; "I have better things to do than to go around the office and disinfect a few hundred stoned PCs!" Without a doubt, viruses are here. Viruses are intentionally designed to damage our computer's software, and they are changing the way we manage our computers.

More than a Nuisance?

Let's start by looking at how we respond to the viral threat. In general, the attitude towards a threat determines the methods used for protection from that threat.

Three responses to the computer viral threat we have seen are: to be awed by the ingenuity of the computer viruses; to sensationalize and exaggerate the viral threat into a computing panic; or to shrug off the potential threat.

The computing community has described viruses in several ways. Some call viruses clever, and yes, some viruses employ well-written code. A virus is a very small program that can hide in memory, take over several aspects of the computer, and self-replicate. Writing a virus does require advanced programming skills and an intimate knowledge of the computer system. Most viruses, however, are not original programs, but slightly modified versions of previous viruses. Norton AntiVirus identifies 1008 strains of 348 viruses.

There is no doubt that some programs deserve praise. Word for Windows' outlining feature, Wing Commander II by Origin, and Sid Meier's Civilization game are worthy of being called clever, and some algorithms (programming code) can be called elegant. But a computer virus, no matter how intelligently written, no matter how tight the code, no matter how unobtrusively a stealth virus hides in memory, never deserves any positive reinforcement.

The media has sensationalized the viral threat to the point of hysteria. Recently, Paul was discussing computing with a friend who is an artist and was considering purchasing her first computer. She was so afraid of computer viruses, she wanted to buy a computer that was "completely blank—never having run any program. Otherwise it may have a virus!"

He assured her, "Viruses are a threat, but they shouldn't stop you from enjoying your computer. Just follow the safe computing tips and your computer will be safe."

Movies like Steven King's *Lawnmower Man* feed the public's fear. Many viewers heard of virtual reality for the first time by watching Jobe transform into a computer hyper-stimulated horror.

Panic and sensationalized stories about computer viruses only serve to further increase the confusion. The sane response to the rogue software threat is simply following safe computing principles.

The third view holds that viruses are no more than a pesky nuisance—"Sure, losing data is expensive, but realistically, no human is actually harmed." The fact is that, unchecked, rogue software can affect human lives.

The novel *RAMA II*, by Arthur C. Clarke, describes a surgery in space that goes awry when the RoSur's (Robotic Surgeon) fault protection is sabotaged. A simple appendectomy becomes the gruesome murder of the space mission's Commanding Officer. Science Fiction? Absolutely.

But today, many medical functions involve computers. Pharmacies use computers to alert them to dangerous drug interactions and drug allergies. Medical scanners (MRI and CAT Scan) use computers to graphically analyze the scan results. Emergency rescue teams use computer links to feed vital signs to doctors in emergency rooms. The nurses' station in intensive care uses centralized life-sign monitoring. Again, these are examples of computers performing life-critical functions. Your physician probably keeps your medical history on a Local Area Network of personal computers. A rogue software attack could easily cost a life.

The list of other *life-critical applications* is also growing: air-traffic control, aircraft autopilots, most communications used for emergencies, and a factory robot's safety features, to name a few. Police are using computer links in police cars for alerts and directions.

I repeat, none of these responses—praising the ingenuity of the virus writers, sensationalizing rogue software until there is panic of digitized fear, or ignoring the potential damage of rogue software—represent a sensible, level-headed approach to computer crime.

Welcome to the World of Computer Vandalism

By definition, rogue software is any program you don't want on your computer. Just as vandalism comes in many forms, so does computer vandalism.

Back Doors

One of the earliest forms of rogue software, a *back door* (also referred to as a *trap door*) is a special password or startup code that is programmed to bypass the normal security. It's not uncommon for a computer program to have a master password so that management can restore a user who has forgotten a password or restore a file that has been encrypted. However, a back door is more than a master password; a back door is a programmer's secret. Some back doors can activate features that the users of the program have no idea exist.

A back door must exist in the *source code*—the program as it's written by the programmer. Another programmer, familiar with the language and project, can usually find a back door in the programming code.

Software can be tested to determine how often each line of code is executed during normal operation of the program. These statistics tell the programmer which part of the program would most benefit from optimization of the code. The security benefit is that this type of analysis will also show code that is not executed normally. That's where to look to find a trap door.

Hollywood Loves Back Doors

In 1983, a back door in the movie *Wargames* took the form of a secret password that bypassed all security. Left behind by the military computer's programmer, the trap door was a secret password, "Joshua," which was the name of his deceased son.

Another movie that hyped back doors is Steven King's *Lawnmower Man*. Jobe learns to fly in the world of virtual reality. As his mind is expanded by the stimulation of virtual reality, he evolves and enters the computer as a virtual-reality being. However, he becomes trapped in the mainframe by a computer virus that takes the mainframe "off the net." Seconds before the whole place blows, the new Jobe finally finds a trap door, and well, we won't give the ending away.

Chameleon

One of the simplest types of rogue software to create, a *chameleon* emulates another program to gather user information. Let's say someone writes a program that looks just like the Novell Netware login text. Instead of logging into Netware, this program collects your username and password. The chameleon program may then run the authentic Netware F:LOGIN, feeding Netware your name and password so that you are logged in and don't suspect a thing.

It is even easier for the chameleon writer to present a seemingly normal error message, such as `File Server Unavailable`. You would probably call the LAN Administrator and complain that the server was down. You would be asked to check your cables and try again. This time the chameleon lets you through. "Sure enough—must have been the cables. LANs are funny about that ya' know."

With a good chameleon, a rogue programmer will know every password on the LAN, minicomputer, or mainframe. Every time a user changes a password, the chameleon program will keep the password list current.

Paul has seen a short batch file compromise every password on a major corporation's Novell Netware LAN. No one noticed it for months.

Logic Bombs

Planted in the program by an angry programmer, *logic bombs* will wait for a certain event (day, command, completion of game, and so on), and then destroy programs and data.

Logic bombs have also been know to be left by contract programmers. If the client paid, the programmers would quietly disarm the logic bomb. If the client refused to pay but continued to use the software, the logic bomb would destroy the software, even if the programmers were denied access to the client's system.

It was a logic bomb that was set to destroy government missile project data at General Dynamics in the summer of 1991. A programmer left the bomb to go off after his resignation. Fortunately, another programmer discovered the bomb and it was disabled.

Trojan Horses

A *Trojan Horse* is a program that acts like a useful utility or entertaining game, but the Trojan Horse adds a "Gotcha!" Just as the Greeks tricked their way into the Trojans's fort by hiding in the gift of a large wooden horse, the Trojan Horse program looks like a gift until the trap is sprung.

An infamous Trojan Horse is the PC/Cyborg AIDS. On December 6, 1988, a fictitious company named PC/Cyborg mailed several thousand diskettes that claimed to contain information on the AIDS virus. Seven thousand of the diskettes were mailed to subscribers of the British computing magazine *PC Business World*, and 3,000 more were mailed to those on a mailing list from an AIDS conference in Stockholm, Sweden.

The PC/Cyborg mailer included a license agreement that, in the fine print, informed the user the software would alter other programs and make the computer unusable. The license agreement also stated that if you used the AIDS program, you would need to lease it for $378, and gave a Panama address.

The mailer included a program AIDS.EXE that presented a survey and estimated your risk of contracting the HIV virus along with lifestyle recommendations to avoid the AIDS virus. The PC/Cyborg installation added a program, REM#, to the AUTOEXEC.BAT file of the unsuspecting user's computer. REM# incremented a counter every time it was executed. When the counter hit 90, the Trojan Horse scrambled the directory structure and created a huge file that filled the remainder of the disk.

The PC/Cyborg mailer was not mailed to the United States. In fact, the survey question "Which country do you live in?" did not include the U.S. as a possible answer. Interestingly, two days after the diskettes began to arrive in Europe, Panama declared war on the United States.

The British computing community quickly spread the word about the PC/Cyborg Trojan Horse, and due to the warnings, few computers were damaged. Although they were not to blame for the mailings, *PC Business World* also quickly sent every subscriber the "AIDSOUT" program that removed the Trojan Horse.

A more recent Trojan Horse was sent around the on-line bulletin boards. A *trainer program,* which allowed a player to cheat at Wing Commander II_XE (an advanced multimedia space combat movie/game by Origin), had been altered to format the disk at the end of the game.

The Twelve Trick Trojan is a nasty program that alters (or *trojanizes*) the boot sector of the hard disk. Originally, a rogue programmer altered copies of CORETEST.COM, version 2.6, (the hard disk benchmark from Core International) to spread the trojan. Recently, it was reported from Canada that the trojan has resurfaced in various shareware programs. The Trojan Horse plays twelve dirty tricks, most that involve randomizing data or placing a random timer delay in some part of DOS. (Although it is not a computer virus, Norton AntiVirus detects and removes the Twelve Trick Trojan.)

ANSI Bombs

Concerning MS-DOS, *ANSI* commonly refers to a set of screen and keyboard control commands specified by the American National Standards Institute. ANSI commands frequently are added to text screens to include color, bold, blinking, and so on. ANSI often is used to add color to the DOS prompt. Paul's DOS prompt uses ANSI graphics to change the color from yellow, for the DOS prompt, to blue for all other text:

```
Prompt $e[40m$e[33m$e[1m$_$p$g$e[36m
```

(The DOS PROMPT command uses $e to represent the escape character [ESC or ACSII 27].)

ANSI also can reconfigure the keyboard, although very few MS-DOS users exploit this aspect of ANSI.SYS. The ANSI sequence, ESC[keyboard code;replacement code;...p, will serve as a keyboard macro writer. The keystroke specified by the keyboard code will send the string rather than the key. The sequence ESC[27;13p or Prompt $e[27;13p$p$g causes the keyboard to send an Enter key whenever you press the Esc key. Most communications software does not use the Esc key. You might not notice the keyboard change until you use the Esc key to back out of a dialog screen and the dialog box's options are accepted instead!

If ANSI.SYS is loaded in CONFIG.SYS, the ANSI sequences do not appear on-screen but simply are executed by ANSI. This can create some wonderful logon screens for bulletin boards. The problem is ANSI commands that reassign the keyboard are also executed without being displayed. You could simply type a text file containing an ANSI bomb to the screen and your keyboard could be altered.

An ANSI bomb can be left in any text that can be displayed by DOS, or any other program that displays ANSI graphics. Several compressed files also now include ANSI graphics at the beginning of the files so that they display a logo when the file is uncompressed. Uncompressing the file would spring the bomb.

Other ANSI bombs are downright mean. They change the screen colors to black on black so you can't see it when you type FORMAT C: <Enter>Y<Enter> when you press the remapped key.

The graphics portion of ANSI has a *clear all* command. Unfortunately, there is no way to clear all keyboard codes. Each code must be reset manually.

If your software begins to act very strangely, you may have been hit by an ANSI bomb. Your program may have received a "2," even though you pressed "3." Fortunately, ANSI codes are temporary and rebooting will erase any ANSI remapping of the keyboard. Once you have removed the ANSI bomb, try to determine which file contains the bomb so that you can delete the file.

I've heard from many computer security experts who are worried about the growth of ANSI bombs. The general public is unaware of this type of rogue software and until recently, there was no way to test for the presence of an ANSI bomb.

Norton AntiVirus, Version 2.0, with virus definition update 2 will check for an ANSI bomb. It's referred to as *ANSI Trojan,* and you need to disable the check executables only option. We also recommend that you forgo using ANSI.SYS, or find a copy of SAFEANSI.SYS, which has the keyboard remap function disabled.

Computer Viruses

Viruses have become the computer terrorism weapon of choice. They hide and spread, becoming a *Trojan Horse upgrade* to your favorite software. There's no need for a virus writer to create a great game in which to hide a Trojan Horse. You don't need to be tempted into downloading the program. You're already sold on using your word processor. That makes the program the perfect carrier for a virus, and makes the virus harder to trace.

Unless you're practicing safe computing and use an antivirus software regularly, you may not know your PC is infected for several months. A *computer virus* is similar to a biological virus. The biological virus attacks a host cell and grows within the host cell until it is ready to explode out of the host and seek other cells to attack.

There is some debate over the technical description of the term *computer virus*. Of the three following definitions, the first definition is technically the most accurate.

- Any program that self-replicates by infecting other programs.

- Any program that self-replicates, including those that make copies of themselves, without infecting a host program.

- V.I.R.U.S, an acronym for *Vital Information Resources Under Siege*, as a generic term, refers to any rogue computer software.

The first definition is the most specific and the most widely accepted. This limits viruses to infecting the following:

- Executable programs (.EXE and .COM files)

- Overlays and drivers (.OVL, .SYS and .DRV)

- DOS (COMMAND.COM and others)

- The startup program in the boot sector or partition table of a disk

One of the primary classifications of viruses is the type of file that the virus will infect. Viruses fall into two broad categories; program infectors and boot sector infectors. COMMAND.COM is listed separately because several program infector viruses only infect COMMAND.COM. Some other program-infecting viruses will infect any program except COMMAND.COM to avoid obvious detection.

In Chapter 2, we will discuss computer viruses in more detail.

Worms

A *worm* is similar to a virus, except that a worm replicates itself as a separate program rather than infecting and hiding in other programs. For example, the Jerusalem virus will infect the program A.EXE, and then it will infect B.EXE, and so on. But a WORM.EXE will find another computer on an attached network and make a copy of WORM.EXE on the second computer. Worms are more prevalent on larger multitasking systems than on the PC.

The *Robert Morris-InterNet* incident that brought 6,000 computers to a halt in 1988 was a worm. It was designed to spread slowly, testing computer system security, but a bug in the worm caused it to spread rapidly, each copy of the worm reinfecting every other computer on the network until the reproduction grew geometrically.

You also should know that *WORM* has another computer-related meaning that refers to an optical disk technology—*Write Once Read Many*.

Droppers

If the virus writer intends to spread the virus quickly, the virus may be given a *dropper program*. A dropper is similar to a Trojan Horse except that it is designed to plant a virus rather than cause destruction by itself. Some viruses (boot-sector viruses) are limited to being spread by the physical passes of diskettes. A dropper program can be written to carry a boot-sector virus in a file and then *plant* it in a target computer.

Who Would Write a Virus?

During the Michelangelo warnings (that seemed to be everywhere the week before March 6, 1992), media interviewers often asked, "Who would do such a thing? Who would create a computer virus?"

The Dawn of Computer Viruses

The World War II era saw the first developments of the electronic computer. During this time, a mathematician, John von Neumann, made great advancements in the area of *artificial intelligence* (or *AI*). AI is the attempt to make computers mimic intelligent thought. One of his concepts was that programs could adapt to their environment, interact with each other, and multiply. Neumann also first presented the idea that software could be destructive towards itself or other software.

The next step in the development of computer viruses was "Core Wars," a high-tech game played after hours by MIT artificial intelligence researchers at AT&T's Bell Laboratories and the Palo Alto Research Center in California. (Early computers used core memory consisting of individual doughnut-shaped iron ferrite "bits" hand wired into memory circuits.) In the game of Core Wars, two programmers would each write a program that would grow within the core memory until it consumed the opposing program. These early games with self-replicating programs were a closely guarded secret until May of 1984 when Core Wars was described in detail in *Scientific American's Computer Recreations* column.

Once it became public knowledge that software could self-replicate, the academic world began to investigate the fascinating new software concept.

Doctor Fred Cohen, then a University of California graduate student, wrote the first modern computer virus in 1983. His demonstration of computer code that could self-replicate eventually earned him a Doctorate in Computer Science. Doctor Cohen was the first researcher to refer to this particular type of software as a "computer virus."

During these early days when universities were experimenting with viruses, a typical virus was the Cookie Monster virus that halted the computer and displayed the message I want a cookie. The computer would be allowed to continue after the user typed the word "cookie."

The budding viruses were primarily experiments in artificial intelligence and an attempt to push the envelope of programming. However, experts became concerned that these software techniques easily could be used for destructive purposes.

Today viral technology is widespread. Examples of viruses, including source code, are readily available to the public. Any programmer who desires to write a virus, easily can find "commented program source code" of popular viruses. Giving a programmer code, complete with comments, is like handing a carpenter a set of plans and a scale model.

In the April 14, 1992 issue of *PC Magazine*, columnist John Dvorak mentioned the proliferation of virus BBSes, including one in Chicago. He says that writing viruses has become a widespread hobby. In support of John's statement is an ad in a 1991 issue of *Popular Science* for The Little Black Book of Computer Viruses, a course in creating viruses. Thus, viruses are being written today by programmers who would otherwise be unable to create a self-replicating program.

The Whiz Kid

Maybe the *whiz kid* is a computer science grad student who desires to make a mark on the world. Often, the whiz kid's intention is benign. The virus, worm, or Trojan Horse is written by a whiz kid to prove to himself that he can do it. The fantasy is to create the ultimate virus, bug-free and impossible to detect. Look at this message left in code inside the Maltese Amoeba virus:

```
AMOEBA virus by the Hacker Twins (C) 1991

This is nothing, wait for the release of AMOEBA II -
The universal infector, hidden to any eye but ours!
```

These whiz kids want to do what no other programmer has done—write the *ultimate virus*; a virus that remains completely undetected until its strike date.

This message brags about the Hacker Twins' next creation. The message is encrypted, it's coded, and it's never displayed. You have to look for the message and look hard to find it. It's a personal taunt, or dare, aimed at all the antivirus researchers.

Maybe the virus gets out of hand. Perhaps it spreads too fast in the Computer Lab. In the previous case of Robert Morris, it was a worm he believed would spread slowly. But it reinfected too quickly and brought 6,000 computers to a halt.

Another virus, the *Semtex virus*, is similar to a screen saver. Other than replicate, it does nothing more than change the screen colors (every character position flashes with a different color randomly) until you press a key that returns the screen to normal. It also includes the following message:

```
S E M T E X by Dusan Toman, CZECHOSLOVAKIA
(7)213-030 or (804)213-23
Karin hat GEBURTSTAG
```

On October 23, the Karin virus displays the message, "Karin has a birthday," in German. Other than the message, this virus does nothing more than replicate.

Fellowship is another replicate-only virus. Other than spreading by infecting programs, the virus does nothing. However, it does contain the following note:

```
This message is dedicated to
all fellow PC users on Earth
Toward A Better Tomorrow
And a better Place To Live In


03/03/90 KV KL MAL
```

Most programmers' first program, as they begin their studies, is a short tutorial program that does nothing more than display "Hello World!" and then ends. The preceding Fellowship virus is the work of a programmer, probably with the initials K.V. living in Kuala Lumpur, Malaysia, who wants to say "Hello World!" with a virus.

In and of themselves, you might think there is little to fault with Semtex or Friendship viruses. They appear to be a friendly greeting of "hello," spread to other programmers who can read inside the virus. A real problem, however, is that the work of the whiz kids becomes the tutorial for the cyberpunks.

Cyberpunks, Crackers, and Hackers

The term *cyberpunk* has been suggested by authors Cliff Stoll in *The Cuckoo's Egg*, and Katie Hafner and John Narkkoff in *Cyberpunk, Outlaws and Hackers on the Computer Frontier*, as a better term to describe the criminal computer subculture than the misused media buzz word "hackers."

The cyberpunk subculture traces its beginning to a 1984 science fiction novel. Case, the anti-hero of William Gibson's *Neuromancer*, is an interface cowboy who runs an earth-wide computer matrix, breaking into computers and stealing data as part of a high tech computer underground. *Neuromancer* has become the legend and inspiration to the entire subculture called cyberpunks.

Pengo, the real life-German cyberpunk whom Cliff Stole caught breaking into several U.S. military computers, stated during his trial that he first got the idea of breaking into computers from *Neuromancer* and John Bunner's *Shockwave Rider*.

The novel *Neuromancer* also has become Neuromancer, the computer game. In the game, you play a cyberpunk, collecting increasingly more powerful software that is used to break into increasingly more secure computer systems.

Hackers are computer enthusiasts who, in a near obsession, strive to squeeze every bit of performance from the computer and the programs they write. They see computing as a lifestyle of efficiency, and hold to the *Hacker Ethic* of clean, elegant design and open information access. Steven Levy's *Hackers—Heroes of the Computer Revolution*, chronicles the hackers from their beginnings at Massachusetts Institute of Technology in the 1960s into the software industry of the 1980s. The Hacker's Ethic has evolved over time and has been influenced by the business of computer software and market pressures.

Some computer professionals find it offensive to call a computer criminal a *hacker*. They feel that hacker should remain a term of respect, honoring a fellow programmer. They have coined another name for a rogue programmer—*cracker*.

Cyberpunks, or crackers, share the hacker's obsession with computers and computer skills, but that's where the similarity ends. The cyberpunk culture is the dark side of hacking. It involves hacking for illegal profit and holds the ultimate task of cracking into a computer system as the highest priority. The cyberpunk's history book also includes a chapter on "Phonephreks," those who are adept at manipulating the phone system and the credit system, often to personally attack an individual.

In the book *Cyberpunk*, the prosecution claims that one of the Cyberpunks actually altered the judge's credit ratings and turned off the probation officer's phones.

The idea of being a part of an adventure runs strong among cyberpunks. During his trial, cyberpunk Pengo told the judge, "The chief thing for me was the adventure, suddenly being inside a movie."

Cyberpunk viruses often contain strains of popular science fiction, fantasy, or comic books. Take a look at the following viral messages. Other popular adventure themes in cyberpunk viruses include:

- Darth Vader—the Darth Vader virus (from *Star Wars*) was one of the first stealth viruses. Rather than adding itself to the end of the infected program, the Darth Vader virus looks for and hides in holes or unused portions of the program to be infected.

- From the very destructive Devil's Dance virus, a taunting message from the movie, *Batman*. As the computer is warm booted (by pressing Ctrl+Alt+Del), the message slowly appears, just before the virus destroys the first copy of the File Allocation Table.

> Have you ever danced with the devil under the weak
> light of the moon? Pray for your disks—the Joker
>
> Ha Ha Ha Ha Ha Ha Ha

- The 4096 virus, with the hidden message FRODO LIVES locks up the computer on September 22. The reference is to Frodo the Hobbit of Tolkien's *Lord of the Rings* trilogy, and September 22 is Bilbo and Frodo Baggin's birthday. On other days the 4096 virus slowly cross-links files.

- !seviL etybwodahS—Shadowbyte Lives! virus read backwards. This name seems to be a cyberpunk take-off from Shadowspawn, a main character of the popular *Thieves World* fantasy series edited by Robert Lynn Asprin, and the novel *Shadowspawn*, by Andrew J. Offutt. Shadowbyte is the Master Thief of Sanctuary— one of the seediest cities in fantasy literature.

Some cyberpunk viruses appear to be practical jokes or pranks, such as the following:

- CRITICAL ERROR 08/15: TOO MANY FINGERS ON KEYBOARD ERROR. The Fingers virus counts the keystrokes. When the key- stroke count hits 3,000 (about 20-30 minutes for an average typist) the message appears and the computer hangs.

- The *F-Word* virus from Russia, inserts the foul phrase, F_ _ _ You!, into every infected file.

- The *Holland Girl* or *Sylvia* virus contains the full name and address of Sylvia V., a girl in Rockanje, Holland. (In respect for Sylvia's privacy, her address is not presented in this book.) Virus "recipients" are asked to send a postcard to Sylvia to receive an antidote. The virus also contains the message This program is infected by a HARMLESS Text-Virus V2.1. I doubt Sylvia views the virus as harmless. It's not known whether Sylvia is the cyberpunk's girlfriend or if this virus is a digital version of bathroom graffiti "For a good time call...."

- A destructive practical joke from Malta, the *Casino* virus makes you play the slot machine—with your hard disk as the stake. DISK DESTROYER.A SOUVENIR OF MALTA I have just

```
DESTROYED the FAT on your Disk!! However, I have a copy
in RAM, and I'm giving you a last chance to restore
your precious data.
```
WARNING: IF YOU RESET NOW, ALL YOUR DATA WILL BE LOST - FOREVER!! Your Data depends on a game of JACKPOT CASINO DE MALTE JACKPOT. If you lose the game, the Casino virus will trash the File Allocation Table of your disk.

The Dark Avenger

A real-life cyberpunk anti-hero goes by the name the *Dark Avenger*. In Bulgaria, he has become very famous among the cyberpunk sub-culture. Most of his viruses are extremely destructive. Two of his viruses corrupt the disk's File Allocation Table very slowly so that the damage is barely noticeable. Once the damage is done, it is nearly impossible to repair the disk. (The Dark Avenger, copyright 1988, 1989. This program was written in the city of Sofia.)

His first virus, the *Dark Avenger* virus, first appeared in Bulgaria during the spring of 1989. It was one of the first "fast-infector" viruses; rather than waiting for a program to be executed before becoming infected, the Dark Avenger virus infects files as they are opened. It even infects files as they are copied. A subtle virus, every 16th time the virus is executed, it overwrites 1 disk sector (512 bytes). Such slow destruction of programs and data is likely to be considered a hardware problem. In the Dark Avenger's first virus he leaves the message Eddie lives... Somewhere in Time!.

Eddie is the "dead dude," a character throughout the albums of heavy metal group Iron Maiden. The *Somewhere in Time* album cover shows Eddie as a sci-fi Cyborg warrior.

Other Dark Avenger viruses also contain references to Iron Maiden, such as *Seventh Son of a Seventh Son*. The *Seventh Son* virus is the title of an album by Iron Maiden. The idea is based on the fantasy novel series by Orson Scott Card. In this fictitious history of colonial America, magic and folklore are more powerful than science. The seventh son has magical power, and Alvin, the seventh son of a seventh son, and a messiah figure, has the magical power to fight the *Unbuilder*.

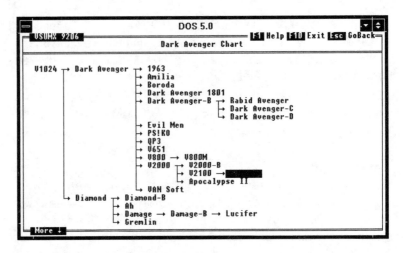

Figure 1-1 VSUM's Dark Avenger virus lineage chart

The *Evil Men* virus, a variant of the Dark Avenger virus, contains the title of a song from the Iron Maiden album, *Seventh Son of a Seventh Son*, "The Evil that Men Do!" The Evil Men virus and the *V800 virus*, both from Bulgaria, also carry an encrypted reference to the title of an Iron Maiden album *Live after Death*. The Dark Avenger also has personally attacked virus researchers. The V2000 or Dark Avenger II virus's message is (c) 1989 by Vesselin Bontchev.

The virus scanner *UScan* claimed to be a universal scanner written by Vesselin Bontchev. It turned out to be a Trojan Horse program that infected every file scanned with the *Anthrax virus*. Vesselin Bontchev is actually Bulgaria's leading anti-virus researcher and Director of the Laboratory of Computer Virology at the Bulgarian Academy of Sciences in Sofia.

The Dark Avenger wrote a variant of the Dark Avenger 4 (V2100 virus), that although not widespread, attempted to trojanize John McAfee's VIRUSCAN, Version 66.

The Dark Avenger's *Mutation Engine* (or DAME according to Spencer Clarke, the SysOp of CompuServe's Computer Virus Help Forum) encrypts or scrambles the code of the virus, making it more difficult to identify the virus.

The Dark Avenger has stated, via electronic mail, that his viruses are so destructive because "destroying data is a pleasure," and that he "just loves to destroy other people's work." Dark Avenger is so self-confident that he recently released a commemorative edition of his first virus, complete with source code.

As this book was going to press, it was reported that the Dark Avenger had been arrested and the Bulgarian BBS, the *Virus eXchange*, had been confiscated. This move marks a dramatic change in the position of the Bulgarian government on computer crimes and a victory for safe computing.

The Terrorist

"Jack [Ryan] pulled out his CIA pass. The guard recognized it for what it was and waved to another guard. This guard punched the button to lower the steel barrier that was supposed to prevent people with car bombs from driving under the headquarters of the FBI. He pulled over it and found a place to park his car. A young FBI agent met him in the lobby and handed him a pass that would work the Bureau's electronic gate. If someone invented the right sort of computer virus, Jack thought, half the government would be prevented from going to work."

—*Clear and Present Danger* by Tom Clancy.

The terrorist commits computer crimes that are politically motivated. These viruses try to remain secret until the activation date when they cause as much destruction as possible. Other political viruses display a message to spread the name of a cause or to discredit or embarrass an opposing viewpoint.

From the Barcelona virus comes the following message:

```
CATALUNYA

CATALUNYA LLIURE

FORA LES FORCES D'OCUPACIO

MORT ALS TERRORISTES TRICORNUTS
```

Catalunya is the area of Spain that includes Barcelona, the host city of the 1992 Summer Olympics. The area of Catalunya has its own language. Following is a rough translation of the viral message:

```
Catalunya cries

for the forces of occupation

death to the tricornuts terrorists
```

Look at the following messages with a cause from other viruses:

- `Green Peace`—GreenPeace virus

- `Europe/92 4EVER!`—Europe-92 virus

- `Dukakis for President`—Dukakis virus (Macintosh)

- `Death to Pascal`—Wisconsin virus (Pascal is a computer programming language.)

The AIDS virus presents the following messages:

- `Your computer is infected with AIDS Virus II`—Signed `WOP & PGT of DutchCrack`—AIDS II virus

- `Getting used to me? Next time, use a Condom...`—More wisdom from the AIDS II virus

Some viruses seem to be religiously motivated.

- `Dark Lord, I summon thee! MANOWAR`—Dark Lord virus

- `*.EXE Xabaras...the name of the devil!! *.COM...Access denied. Your PC has been infected by XABARAS VIRUS, created by Cracker Jack 1991 (c) IVRL`—Xabaras Virus was written by Cracker Jack, an Italian cyberpunk

- `Kampanya Anti-Telefonica. Menos tarifas y mas servicio. Programmed in Barcelona (Spain). 23-8-90.` Virus Anti—C.T.N.E. v2.10a. (c)1990 Grupo Holokausto.

- `666`—Holocaust virus

The Telefonica or Telecom was written by the same individual who wrote the Holocaust virus. Both cause damage data; the Telecom actually wipes the hard disk clean. The Holocaust virus is considered a stealth virus; however, the Telecom waits for the infected computer to be booted 400 times before activating, which in my mind is more devious. It is rumored that the Telecom virus is a protest against high telephone rates in Spain.

Revenge plays a part of the most destructive viruses. Earlier, we saw the first part of the Maltese Amoeba virus as an example of the virus writer's fantasy of writing the ultimate virus. Now look at the rest of the Hacker Twins' hidden message:

```
Dedicated to the University of Malta-the worst

educational system in the universe, and the destroyer

of 5X2 years of human life

- Maltese Amoeba
```

Clearly, this is a virus motivated by revenge. When it strikes on November 1 and March 15, it effectively trashes the hard disk by overwriting the first 4 sectors of the first 30 cylinders of the hard disk. Then it displays the following message:

```
To see a world in a grain of sand,

And a heaven in a flower

Hold infinity in the palm of your hand

And eternity in an hour.

THE VIRUS 16/3/91
```

Originally, researchers believed the Maltese Amoeba, common in Ireland and England, would strike on November 5, which is Guy Fawkes Day. (In 1605 Guy Fawkes was seized for an attempt to blow-up the Houses of Parliament.) Edward Wilding of the Virus Bulletin in England said, "We were certainly taken by surprise."

Perhaps the most famous terrorist virus is the *Jerusalem virus*, specifically designed by terrorists to inflict economic damage on Israel. The virus strikes on any Friday the 13th, but the significance isn't the normal bad luck associated with Friday the 13th. Friday, May 13, 1988, was the fortieth anniversary of the end of the Palestine State.

The Researcher

This topic is classified.

Rumors claim that the National Security Agency develops advanced viruses as future weapons. It was also rumored that America used some type of rogue software to shut down the Iraqi air defense system moments before the start of the Desert Storm air war. There is no hard evidence to substantiate either suspicion.

On October 6, 1991, the *New York Times* reported that the U.S. Army has appropriated $550,000 for research into computer viruses as military weapons. Military computer systems tend to be closely guarded with no outside access. It seems very unlikely that we could have stopped a missile strike by releasing a virus into the old U.S.S.R.'s missile command. This topic reminds me of the old joke—"I could tell you, but then I'd have to shoot you...."

Where in the World is Carmen Sandiego?

World-traveler Carmen Sandiego perhaps is the most infamous of all computer criminals. She and her band of thieves have eluded the Acme Crime Busters in several of Borderbund's Carmen Sandiego games. The best seller is being used in most schools and has been transformed into a popular Public Service Television afterschool game show. Just like Carmen Sandiego, viruses come from all over the globe.

Sometimes it's clear where the virus was written. The writer of the virus leaves a message or even a copyright notice. Some viruses are very common in only one area, so it's logical to conclude that the virus is local to the infestation. Some viruses are clearly the work of the same virus author as other known viruses. All these clues and more are used by virus researchers to piece together the origin and lineage of viruses.

Virus Count by Country of Origin or Discovery

50	Bulgaria	3	Czechoslovakia
44	United States	3	England
38	USSR (former)	3	India
24	Italy	3	Indonesia
22	Germany	3	Portugal
19	Poland	3	Sweden
18	Canada	2	Austria
18	Netherlands	2	Denmark
18	New Zealand	2	Greece
14	Taiwan	2	Malaysia
12	Israel	2	Malta
11	Spain	2	Philippines
8	Republic of South Africa	2	Thailand
8	Saudi Arabia	1	Belgium
7	Australia	1	Bolivia
7	Hungary	1	Hong Kong
5	Finland	1	Ireland
5	Switzerland	1	Korea
4	France	1	Mexico
4	Iceland	1	Pakistan
3	Argentina		

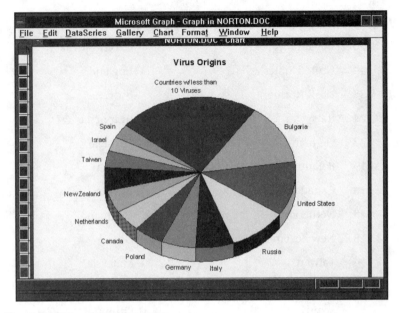

Figure 1-2 Virus origins by country

Bulgaria—The Virus Plague

You may have noticed that the number one producer of computer viruses is Bulgaria. According to Vesselin Bontchev, Director of the Laboratory of Computer Virology at the Bulgarian Academy of Sciences in Sofia, Bulgaria, following are reasons for the large number of viruses written in Bulgaria:

- A huge army of angry, young, and extremely qualified computer programmers who are underpaid and unappreciated.

- No computer software copyright laws—"The lack of respect to the others' work is a common problem in the socialist societies." Software piracy is a state policy. Because software is not protected, damaging software with a virus is not considered a crime. Writing viruses has been completely legal in Bulgaria; however, the recent arrest of the Dark Avenger may indicate a change in this position.

- The economy is so slow and software piracy so common that there is no chance of selling software to earn a living. "This caused several young people to become embittered against the society that was unable to evaluate them as it should. There is only one step in the transformation of these young people into creators of destructive viruses. Some of them (e.g., the Dark Avenger) took this step."—Vesselin Bontchev

- There is no organized struggle against viruses in Bulgaria; however, the cyberpunks are organized. The Virus eXchange, BBS, and other bulletin board services, make viral source codes available to anyone who uploads a new virus. Virus tricks and detailed information about manipulating MS-DOS freely flow through the cyberpunk network. A popular file is *INTERxyy*, by Ralf Brown (USA), which carefully describes a huge number of undocumented tricks.

Most of the viruses written in Bulgaria do not leave the country. Several virus writers claim that they never let their viruses go wild. However, these writers do send copies of their viruses to United States virus researchers so that they can see their virus added to the antivirus list and claim any virus reward offered. According to Vesselin Bontchev, only one in ten Bulgarian viruses are successfully spread outside of Bulgaria.

The Bulgarians write some of the most advanced viruses. Four of the six smallest viruses listed in Patricia Hoffman's *Virus Information Summary List* are from Bulgaria, the smallest being only 30 bytes long. That's smaller than this sentence.

The Russian Viruses

Bulgaria may have been the leading producer of computer viruses, but the new Commonwealth of Independent States is quickly overtaking it. Some virus surveys of new viruses already show Russia ahead of Bulgaria. At the Fourth Annual Computer Virus & Security Conference on March 15, 1991, Klaus Brummstein of the University of Hamburg said that Russia has replaced Bulgaria as the leading source of computer viruses.

```
Victor V1.0 The Incredible High Performance Virus

Enhanced versions available soon.

This program was imported from USSR.

Thanks to Ivan.

—The Victor virus
```

There may even be a rivalry developing between Bulgarian and Russian virus writers. Take a look at the following message from the Russian virus, *Red Diavolyata*:

```
Eddie die somewhere in time

This program was written in the city of Prostokwashino

(C) 1990  RED DIAVOLYATA

Hello! MLTI!
```

Either the author of the Red Diavolyata virus doesn't appreciate heavy metal music or this is an aggressive retort to Bulgaria's Dark Avenger.

In October of 1991, *Newsbytes* reported that the Driver-1024 virus, from Bulgaria, "had infected 20 percent of the PCs in Moscow, including ones in the KGB facilities."

The Russian and Bulgarian threat isn't the *quantity* of viruses. The threat is the increasing complexity and stealth capabilities of the virus. At least three of the worst new stealth viruses come from the Russian/Bulgarian area: the *SVC 6*, *DIR II*, and the *Pogue* virus. John Dvorak recently wrote in *PC Magazine*, "bored programmers in Russia and Bulgaria are the main source of this new [stealth] viral technology."

It is our hope that political reform and economic improvement can bring Russia and Bulgaria out of their current status as a cyberpunk virus breeding ground.

Michelangelo

In March of 1992, computer viruses became a part of the mainstream American life. Our first real celebrity virus had arrived on the scene. Every newspaper, radio show, and TV news that you could find covered the *Michelangelo* virus warnings. Some extended the coverage to mention safe computing or the other two viruses that strike hard every March. The headline of the *Wall Street Journal* (March 6, 1992) summed up the emotion:

High-Tech Hysteria Grips Nation; SkyLab? No, the Michelangelo Virus.

The Media Event

This certainly is a virus that did its public relations work. The name *Michelangelo* invokes a sense of culture. The Renaissance period was filled with creativity, passion, and art. Michelangelo presents the visual media (TV, cable, and print) with a multitude of eye-catching images for all generations. From the Sistine Chapel to the Teenage Mutant Ninja Turtles, the general public could relate to Michelangelo's visual appeal. The virus activates on the 517th birthday of the Renaissance artist. As a nation, we love commemorative events.

It is far better "good copy" with mass audience appeal to discuss the Michelangelo virus on "Good Morning America!" than it would be to demonstrate the Stoned virus. Names, such as 1575, 4096, 5120, Cascade-B, Dark Avenger, Dir-2, Disk Killer, Dutch 555, Invader, Possessed, or Slayer Family, are just not vibrant enough for the 6 p.m. news.

Michelangelo doesn't play games either; when it strikes, it effectively unpartitions the hard disk. The only recourse is to reformat and restore from backups.

Even the Lone Star State got some positive "PR" from Michelangelo; as Texans on CompuServe claimed, if they, rather than the Europeans, had discovered the virus, the Michelangelo virus would have been dubbed the "Alamo virus."

As the virus trigger date approached, every news show in America covered the threat. ABC's "Nightline" devoted an entire show to Michelangelo, even demonstrating Norton AntiVirus.

Leading Edge computers shipped PCs infected with the virus. Paul personally saw Michelangelo appear on the diskettes used to format and build the hard drives of new PCs at two PC service centers.

On March 5, 1992, the day before Michelangelo struck, newspapers were full of dire predictions. As the hysteria mounted, estimates of the number of infected DOS computers rose higher and higher. Last-minute press stories covered mobs at computer software stores clamoring for the last few copies of antivirus utilities.

The Aftermath

March 6 saw the results of the widespread Michelangelo panic; the warnings paid off. As few as 2,000 computers were affected worldwide. Most of those hit were outside the United States. The Republic of South Africa was the hardest hit with about 1,000 PCs affected, primarily their heath care industry, a hospital, and pharmacies.

We may never know how many computers were infected by Michelangelo. Some estimates go as high as 5 million infected PCs. The Norton AntiVirus Technical Support estimate is more conservative, at about 60,000.

The best result of the Michelangelo scare was that most PC users became aware of the viral threat and started to protect their PCs. Because computer viruses made the front page of the *Wall Street Journal*, corporate management began to take viruses seriously.

It turned out that Michelangelo was a big shot of anti-virus in the computing community's arm. It was common to hear, "We checked all our office PCs for Michelangelo. Didn't find him but we found two Stoned viruses and a Jerusalem virus."

Two other viruses were set to trigger during March of 1992. The Jerusalem virus hits every Friday the 13th, and the Maltese Amoeba strikes November 1 and March 15. The Jerusalem virus has caused significant damage in the past; however, most recently, very little damage was reported (perhaps due to the virus cleaning prompted by Michelangelo). There were no reports of the Maltese Amoeba striking in the U.S.

Common Virus Myths

Rogue software is surrounded with myth and misconception. From BBS text files about viruses, computer magazine articles, newspapers and conversations, we've collected a few of the more interesting false-hoods being circulated about computer viruses and rogue software.

Myth #1: I Won't Get a Virus

Eventually, you will see a virus, even if you never swap diskettes or files. New computers and shrink-wrapped commercial software have been documented to contain viruses. According to virus fighter Jim Jester, computer technicians, service centers, and computer stores account for about 60 percent of viruses spread in the United States. He attributes the remaining 40 percent to users sharing diskettes and files.

This is not meant to scare you. If you follow the guidelines for safe computing in Chapter 3, you will avoid any damage to your computer the virus writer may have intended.

If you are not practicing safe computing, however, chances are that sooner or later you may experience computer problems from some type of rogue software.

Myth #2: Data Files Can Be Infected

A virus can try to infect a *data file*, but the virus would no longer work. The data file would become corrupt, perhaps unrecognizable by your application program. The virus instruction codes that were written to the data file would never be executed. Also, DOS does not run a data file as a program.

Can data files be *affected* by a virus? Absolutely. *Infected*? No. Could a virus write program code to the beginning of a data file thereby turning it into a rogue program? Maybe.

Keep in mind that data diskettes can carry viruses in the boot sector of the diskette.

Myth #3: If I Get a Virus, I'll Know It

Maybe. Norton AntiVirus Technical Support says that only four viruses account for 85 percent of their phone calls. In descending order, they are the Stoned, Jerusalem, Michelangelo, and Joshi viruses. Other surveys show the Stoned virus responsible for 60 percent of all computer virus infections. The Stoned virus displays the message Your computer is now stoned., and the Joshi virus says Happy Birthday Joshi. Neither virus destroys data.

On the other hand, the Jerusalem virus was created as a political weapon, and most versions will hide until Friday the 13th, when they destroy files. Michelangelo also will remain quiet until March 6, when simply turning on and booting your computer completely erases your hard disk. What about the other 15 percent of the viruses? You'll find information about them elsewhere in this book. Some viruses display messages; however, most do not. Of those viruses that are destructive, unless you are using antivirus software, you wouldn't notice many of them until it's too late.

So the sage answer as to whether you'll know if your computer gets a virus is "No." You are not safe if you wait until you see a sign of a virus and then belatedly follow the safe computing guidelines.

Myth #4: BBSs Spread Viruses

Wrong. Three of the four most common viruses are boot sector viruses and cannot be sent over a phone line as an infected file. (Boot sector viruses don't infect programs. They only infect a diskette or the boot sector of a disk, and are spread by sharing infected diskettes.)

This isn't by chance. Boot sector viruses outnumber file-program infecting viruses because BBSes catch the program-infecting viruses. The BBS SysOp cannot keep you from carrying an infected diskette home from work.

Bulletin boards do more to spread the *awareness* of viruses than they spread viruses. The primary method of communication concerning viruses is through BBSes. On a national level, there are four primary virus-fighting BBSes ready to help you, the Norton AntiVirus user.

- The Norton AntiVirus section of the Symantec/Norton Utilities Forum on CompuServe (Go NorUtl)

- Symantec/Norton BBS

- Excaliber by Patricia Hoffman

- Virus Help Forum from CompuServe

These BBSes answer questions about new viruses and using Norton AntiVirus. They disseminate virus-signature updates and provide instant feedback to the developers about how Norton AntiVirus is working in the field.

> **NOTE:** For the record—being connected to a BBS will not infect your computer. You must download and run an infected file for your computer to become infected. Also, merely being connected to a computer via a phone line cannot infect your computer. It is nothing but a rumor that 9600 baud communications uses a 300 baud subcarrier capable of transmitting a virus undetected.

Within any local phone call area, there are probably two to twenty BBSes. Most BBS SysOps are careful about scanning newly uploaded files for viruses. If their board earns a reputation for spreading tainted software, they would quickly lose their good patrons. Some BBS programs even include the capability to scan for viruses automatically.

Most importantly, the local BBS is like the local "pub of old." Computer users regularly discuss problems and tips "on the board." If there is a computer virus spreading around your city, a local BBS is where you will hear about it.

There are pirate BBSes. Their purpose is to spread *cracked* software (commercial software with the serial number or copy protection removed). The pirate BBS SysOps are very secretive about who knows the BBS phone number, and the pirated software often is in private areas of the BBS so that the average user doesn't see the illegal files. The pirate boards often maintain a section of computer virus available for downloading. You should always avoid pirated software. Beyond the moral and legal issues, pirated software often is exposed to computer viruses.

Myth #5: Backups Are Useless Against a Virus

A backup is the best last defense against any computer problem, including computer viruses. Even if every backup set contains a virus-infected program, you can still selectively restore your data files.

Some viruses corrupt data slowly. If your backup plan doesn't allow for long backup periods or grandfather backups, it is possible that your backup set contains bad data. Chapter 3, "Strategies for Safe Computing," suggests a backup plan.

Myth #6: Computers Just Aren't Safe Anymore—They Are a Security Threat to Society

The term for this belief is *cyberphobia*—the fear of computing. The idea is that by becoming dependent on computing, our society is at the mercy of anyone with a PC. A cyberphobe might say, "Computer whizzes are infiltrating the banks daily and stealing us all blind. And of course the banks never even know about the theft because they can't count the change of a ten dollar bill without using a computer."

The idea that computer security is bypassed easily by every whiz kid is fueled by what you might call the *McGyver Syndrome*. On TV and in the movies, a technically inclined individual (especially McGyver) can walk up to any computer, break past the security in about 30 seconds, and connect instantly to every other computer in the world. It is true, as a culture we have grown dependent on computing—and gasoline, and phones, and TV—our total infrastructure. The same fear of change more than likely resisted the concept of currency when coins first began to replace the barter system. The fact is that military computers are much more secure than the media portrays. They are even safe from McGyver.

Myth #7: A Good Virus?

Recently, there has been a question about the possibility of *good viruses*. The benign-virus theory states that "computer viruses are a technology, neither good nor evil in itself." So far, computer viral technology has been used primarily as pranks, but if humankind could harness viral technology, it could serve for the good. A good virus could silently spread software upgrades throughout a network. A benign worm could seek persons on the network that meet a certain criteria, delivering specialized E-mail. The "good virus" theory even proposes a virus version of antivirus software that combats the evil viruses as they spread.

The problem with such a scheme is that it ignores the issues of privacy and control. You own your computer, and no one has the right to "silently" upgrade your software or search your E-mail.

A related myth is that computer viruses represent a major step towards "artificial life." Wrong. Computer viruses merely are programs that copy themselves. They do not advance the cause of artificial intelligence, robotics, or "artificial life."

Myth #8: Destructive Computer Programs Are a Relatively New Thing

The human capacity for destruction has been known since the dawn of time. Computer viruses are new, but Trojan Horses have been around since the beginning of programming.

Myth #9: Viruses Are Reaching Epidemic Levels

Well, that all depends on how epidemic is defined.

The virus problem is growing. The best estimate is that about 16 to 20 percent of the PCs in the United States have been infected. If you are very active in personal computing, you are likely to see a virus. However, the term *virus epidemic* involves more than just how widespread a problem has become. An epidemic is something out of control, with no immediate hope of a solution.

There is a solution to the viral threat. Safe computing can significantly reduce the chance that your computer will be affected by rogue software. We'd like to promise you a zero percent chance, but that would be testing fate. We can promise that if you follow the guidelines to safe computing, you will minimize the chances of data damage from a virus attack significantly.

Myth #10: Antivirus Software Is Virtually Useless—1,000 New Viruses Are Discovered Each Year

Due to programming errors, many viruses that are written don't replicate or activate properly, so they die right away. Of the working viruses that are planted and begin to spread, four out of five never reach the point of critical mass required for the infection to spread beyond a few dozen computers. Half of the viruses that begin to spread are discovered quickly and—having been discovered—are identified and removed.

For the few viruses that are left, with any luck, someone will notice the virus and report it. Once the antivirus industry provides protection against the new virus, its spread can be halted.

This myth's second assumption is that there is no defense against a new virus. This simply is not true. Norton AntiVirus, and other antivirus utilities, can easily detect a change in a file indicating an unknown virus.

Myth #11: A PC Virus Might Take Down the Mainframe

A virus is a program. A program for one computer generally cannot be run to a different type of computer. The instruction sets of two different CPU families are completely foreign to each other. Macintosh programs can't run on a PC. DEC Vax software doesn't run on an IBM AS-400.

This incompatibility presents a problem for legitimate computer-software developers who write programs for many types of computers. The program has to be designed and then rewritten for each type of computer. While there are tools and languages that make "porting" a program from one computer system to another possible, this task often is difficult.

Viruses function at such a low level, closely tied to operating system and nonstandard hardware functions, that porting a computer virus would be nearly impossible. It is impossible for the same virus to infect two dissimilar computer systems. There has been one exception: a virus that could infect two different types of *UNIX_XE* operating-system computers. A virus that infects MS-DOS style personal computers, however, could not infect a minicomputer or mainframe computer.

Theoretically, (very theoretically), a PC virus could be used as a dropper program to carry a second virus (actually, mainframe computers have more problems with computer worms than computer viruses) that infects a different type of computer. Such a design is extremely impractical, and it would be difficult for the virus to ever connect up with the correct type of secondary computer.

More than likely, you would configure a portion of your mainframe's disk storage as a PC fileserver for a local area network. Infected programs could be stored in this area or the mainframe. You can assure your data-processing manager, however, that the mainframe has a better chance of running MS-Windows 3.1 than becoming infected by a PC computer virus that resides in the PC disk storage area (i.e. virtually zero).

Myth #12: A Read-Only File Is Safe from Virus Infection

The October 1991 issue of *PC Magazine* included a major review of antivirus software. A sidebar, *Five Common-Sense Tips for Safer Computing*, actually stated that setting the executable files as read-only with the DOS ATTRIB command would "help contain those [viruses] that attack executable files."

Under MS-DOS, for security, files can be set as *read-only*, *system*, or *hidden*. The read-only setting normally stops a program or DOS command from deleting or writing to the file. Changing the read-only setting is as easy as changing a bit from 1 to 0. The DOS command, ATRIB-R filename, easily changes the read-only bit. The read-only bit is a piece of cake for a virus to change or bypass. It doesn't even slow the virus down.

To prove this, Paul set a test program (the DOS MEM.EXE program) to read-only, suspended Norton AntiVirus's virus protection, and then infected the PC with the Jerusalem virus. It's a very common file-infecting virus that will infect any program that is run while the virus is active. When the MEM program was executed, sure enough Jerusalem promptly infected it. The read-only bit was still set to true after the program was altered. The virus simply changed the read-only bit, infected the file, and then restored the read-only bit.

Despite what computer magazines may print, the "read-only" method of protection is comparable to locking your house with a zipper.

Myth #13: A Nasty Virus Might Get Past the Write-Protect Tab on a Diskette

Related to the read-only bit, which is a software method of write-protecting a file, is the write-protect tab of a diskette.

5 1/4-inch diskettes can be protected from accidental disk writes by placing a tab over a notch. 3 1/2-inch diskettes contain a built-in sliding tab for write-protection. The practice is similar to breaking off the write-protect tab on a VCR tape or audio cassette tape. The diskette drive uses a small light to see if the diskette has been write-protected. If the diskette is write-protected, the drive's electronics keep it from writing to the diskette. There is no program or virus that could alter the electronic design of the diskette drive and bypass the diskette write protection.

Viruses are software and can only affect software. A virus cannot physically change the electronic design of your computer.

Myth #14: A Virus Can Damage the Computer Hardware

This is a myth that has a touch of reality. It is possible for software to command the hardware to operate outside of its designed limits. For example, it is possible for software to instruct a hard disk to move beyond the disk's normal stops, potentially damaging the drive heads. Another example would be changing the video card settings to damage a monitor.

Today, there is no virus that attempts these activities. The multi-vendor environment of the PC world would make attempting such a virus impractical. Such a virus would be very machine specific. Chances would be that what causes damage to your friend's computer wouldn't hurt your computer. Early diagnostic software did occasionally test the PC beyond its limits and caused hard drive problems, but today there is no such threat.

When you hear that a virus "zaps" a hard drive or wipes out a machine, the damage is all to the software. The hard disk can be restored. It may take a reformat or even a low-level format, but the hardware of the machine is still usable.

Myth #15: To Avoid a Date-Activated Virus, Just Change the Date on the Computer

Isn't this similar to letting one horse out of the barn, and then closing the barn door when the barn is on fire?

As a last minute precaution, changing the date is better than getting hit by a virus, but you still need to deal with the virus. Changing the date is a temporary cheat.

Summary

Computer vandalism is out there. Somewhere in the world, a programmer is losing sleep creating a new way to corrupt software and destroy data. The most reasonable reaction to this criminal threat is to prepare for it and keep on computing.

There are many types of rogue software: back doors, Trojan Horses, droppers, chameleons, logic bombs, ANSI bombs, worms, and viruses. Of all of these, viruses represent the greatest threat because they replicate, transforming your favorite software into a Trojan Horse.

The programmers who write rogue software are as varied as the many types of criminal code; early researchers pushing toward artificial intelligence, the whiz kids proving that they can do it too, the cyberpunks lashing back at society, and the true terrorists using rogue software as an economic weapon.

Rogue software is surrounded by myths and rumors. Dispelling these myths and understanding the true nature of the beast is the first step toward eliminating it.

Bibliography

Alexander, Michael. *Infection risk not spurring use of antivirus software.* ComputerWorld, 1991.

Bontchev, Vesselin. *The Bulgarian and Soviet Virus Factories.* unpublished paper, 1991

Clancy, Tom. *Clear and Present Danger.* Berkley Publishing, 1989.

Clarke, Arthur C. and Gentry Lee. *RAMA II.* Bantam Books, 1989.

Dvorak, John C. *The Future of the Virus.* PC Magazine, Ziff Davis Publishing Corp., 1991.

Dvorak, John C. *The New Stealth Viral Threat.* PC Magazine, Ziff Davis Publishing Corp., 1992.

Ellison, Carol. *Five Common Sense Tips for Safer Computing.* PC Magazine, Ziff Davis Publishing, 1991.

Ellison, Carol. *On Guard: 20 Utilities that Battle the Viral Threat.* PC Magazine, Ziff Davis Publishing, 1991.

Gibson, William. *Neuromancer.* Berkley Publishing Group, 1984.

Glath, Raymond M. *Computer Viruses: A Rational View.* unpublished paper, 1988

Greeley, Andrew M. *God Game.* TOR Books, 1986.

Hafner, Katie and John Markoff. *Cyberpunk: Outlaws and Hackers on the Computer Frontier.* Simon and Schuster, 1991.

Haibloom, Cory. *Learning about MS-DOS Viruses.* Norton AntiVirus Training Materials, Symantec/Peter Norton Group, 1992.

Hambly, Barbara. *The Silicon Mage.* Random House, 1988.

Hoffman, Patricia M. *The Virus Information Summary List in HyperText, February 1992.* 1990-1992.

Kane, Pamela. *Avoiding Viruses.* WordPerfect Publishing Corp, 1991.

Lethal Virus Takes Busters by Surprise. PC User News, EMAP Business & Computer Publications, 1991.

Levin, Richard B. *The Computer Virus Handbook.* Osborne McGraw-Hill, 1990.

Levy, Steven. *Hackers—Heroes of the Computer Revolution.* Dell Publishing, 1991

McAfee, John and Colin Haynes. *Computer Viruses, Worms, Data Diddlers, Killer Programs, and Other Threats to Your System.* St. Martin's Press, 1989.

Minasi, Mark. *Computer Viruses from A to Z.* Compute Magazine, Computer Publications International, 1991.

Molloy, Maureen. *Top Level Backing Key to Virus Defense.* Network World, 1991.

Rosenberger, Rob and Ross M. Greenberg. *Computer Virus Myths.* unpublished paper, 1992.

Solomon, Dr. Alan, Barry Nielson, and Simon Meldrum. *The AIDS Trojan.* unpublished paper, 1989.

Solomon, Dr. Alan. *Twelve Tricks Trojan Report.* unpublished paper, 1990.

Stoll, Cliff. *The Cuckoo's Egg.* Doubleday, 1989.Sullivan, Kristina B. *Virus Policies Vary Widely.* PC Week, Ziff Davis Publishing, 1991.

Tchashchin, Kirill. *New Viruses Hit Moscow.* Newsbytes Inc., 1991.

Numerous newspaper articles from the following publications:

Charlotte Observer, 1992

Hickory Daily Record, 1992

Miami Herald, 1992

New York Times, 1991, 1992

Orlando Sentinal, 1992

USA Today, 1992

Wall Street Journal, 1990, 1991, 1992

A Closer Look at Viruses

The computer virus panic has caused confusion and has even blurred the term "computer virus." In the last chapter, three popular definitions of the term "virus" were presented:

- A program that self-replicates by infecting other programs.

- Any program that self-replicates, including those that make copies of themselves without infecting a host program.

- V.I.R.U.S., an acronym for "Vital Information Resources Under Siege"; used as a generic term, V.I.R.U.S. refers to any rogue computer software.

This first definition is a true computer virus.

Virus definition two is actually a *worm*.

Definition number three is completely inaccurate and only serves to cloud the understanding of rogue software and computer security.

Now we'll take a detailed look at computer viruses, and how they reproduce. The three most prominent viruses will be examined closely. What is more important, we'll reveal the inherent weaknesses in viruses, on which Norton AntiVirus's attack strategy is based.

Basic Virus Information

The term "computer virus" comes from their resemblance to biological viruses. So first, let's briefly review a fascinating topic you probably haven't seen since high school.

Biological Viruses

A *biological virus* is an infectious parasite cell that attacks a host cell, and then reproduces itself within the structure of that same host cell (see figure 2-1).

Following is a list of biological virus traits:

- Very small, only 100–300 nanometers (a fraction of the size of the host cell)

- Simple in composition as compared to the host organism

- Requires an animal, plant, or bacterial cell in which to grow

- Vary in their morphology (form and structure)

- Very short life cycle. Biological viruses reproduce in only 20 to 45 minutes. That's roughly .0000005 percent—as long as the life of the organism being infected.

- Spread in many diverse ways from the noninvasive (moisture in the air) to the invasive (blood transfusions)

- The host organism develops specialized antibodies that attack and destroy the specific infecting virus

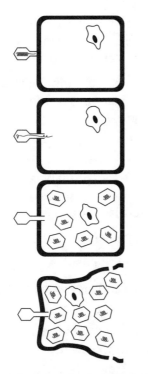

Virus contacts cell

Injects nucleic acid
into cell

Cell duplicates
the virus

Destroyed cell
bursts, releasing
new viruses to
infect other cells

Figure 2-1 Reproductive cycle of a biological virus

Computer Viruses

Computer viruses resemble biological viruses in several aspects. Computer viruses are also incredibly small compared to the programs they infect. Computer viruses are commonly between 1024 and 2048 bytes, with the smallest computer virus being only 30 bytes long. 1Kb, for instance, is about 1 percent the size of the entire Norton AntiVirus. Microsoft's Word for Windows is about 11 million times larger.

Computer viruses also are particular about infecting only certain types of host programs on specific computer systems. They do not execute themselves but depend on the host program's execution to activate or run the computer virus. Computer viruses reproduce very swiftly compared to the life of a computer or even the installation process of most application software, and sometimes destroy their host program or their host computer's entire software.

Also, just like their biological counterparts, computer viruses are combated by identifying the virus and developing antidotes or specific software to remove the virus infection.

Computer viruses generally fall into two groups: those that infect files, and those that infect disk or diskette boot sectors. A third category, *stealth viruses*, is a subset of the two primary categories, and its category types describe the virus's various methods of avoiding detection. Following are the primary viral classifiers:

- Name of the virus name and any aliases

- Type of files the virus infects and the method of infection

- Geographical origin of the virus and also when and where it was first discovered or isolated

- Length of the virus in bytes; the length may also include the amount of infected file growth as well as the size of the virus while loaded in memory

- How widespread the virus infectious has become

- Noticeable symptoms

- Activation trigger that causes the virus to display the symptoms or damage

- Damage the virus may inflict on any files on the disk, or any negative effects on the operation of the computer

The life of a computer virus (life cycle of computer viruses) is best examined in two cycles. The life cycle is a larger cycle that involves the global spread and effect of the virus. This cycle begins with the virus's programming, and continues through the spread of the virus until it is finally eliminated by the computing community. The *reproductive cycle* involves the viral infection of an increasing number of host programs.

A computer virus's reproductive cycle and its efficiency vary with the type of virus. Program-infecting viruses usually reproduce by infecting other programs that are being executed. Some program-infecting viruses are *fast infectors* and can infect a program if the program's file is read from the disk regardless of whether or not the program is executed.

Boot sector viruses spread by infecting the boot sectors of diskettes. When infected diskettes are shared between one or more computers, the newly exposed computer's hard disk becomes infected from the shared diskette.

Computer Virus Life Cycles

The virus's life cycle is the long-term infectious spread of the virus and typically is one to three years long. A simple analysis of the virus life cycle shows four common phases.

Launch Phase

The *launch phase* is the initial design and programming of the virus and the release of the virus into the wild. Viruses are often first discovered in university computer labs, on international BBSes, or on specific networks. The location in which a virus is first isolated is sometimes far from the virus's true origin. For example, Bulgaria's *Dark Avenger* was known to have called BBSes in Denmark and Germany to release viruses.

Until recently, when the Anti-Viral Product Developer's Consortium of the National Computer Security Association appointed Patricia Hoffman (author of *VSUM*) as the official virus librarian, cataloging computer viruses had been a major problem. Some viruses received multiple names as they were independently identified by several anti-virus researchers. This tendency towards many virus names and aliases contributes to the confusion and the falsehoods that surround computer viruses.

The virus-name chaos has even confused *PC/Computing Magazine*. A recent *PC/Computing* "Fax Poll" identified the top six viruses as: Stoned, Jerusalem, Azusa, Hong Kong, Music Bug, and Friday the 13th. One of the problems is that Friday the 13th is both a virus and an alias for the widespread Jerusalem virus. The Azusa and Hong Kong viruses are one and the same!

Initial Spread Phase

During the *initial spread phase*, the virus infection is small and often geographically localized. This would be similar to the early stages of a biological infection, when the virus is beginning to *take root* in the host organism but has not yet reached a sufficient level to cause symptoms or to alert the natural antibodies. It is this quiet before the storm that allows the virus to spread.

Keep in mind that the rogue programmer can launch or release the virus several times in several different locations, giving the virus a substantial boost during the initial spread phase.

The more deadly viruses are programmed in an attempt to spread as quietly as possible during this initial stage. If a virus caused strong ill effects or damaged software the very first time it was executed, the virus would quickly be caught and would not have the opportunity to spread. Most viruses delay their symptoms to give the virus time to spread the infection as wide as possible before striking.

The Michelangelo virus spreads without any obvious symptoms, and then one day, it destroys the hard disk. The other widely spread virus that causes damage, the Jerusalem virus, only deletes files on any Friday the 13th, or about once every seven months.

Viruses developed for research present another aspect of the development/launch phase. Research viruses are developed for research and are not intended to be released into the wild. However, virus-research authors routinely send a sample of the virus to the virus library for cataloging so that the public can be prepared if the virus is accidentally released. Several "research viruses" have appeared on United States pirate BBSes. By definition, a research virus has had no reports of infection in the wild. However, the easy availability of many research viruses means several computer crackers or virus collectors will soon have copies of research viruses. A research virus encounter in the wild is inevitable.

Ideally, the antivirus industry would like to isolate the virus during this early initial phase, before the virus has done significant damage. While the virus spread is small, it is possible to provide antivirus protection and keep the virus in the "rare" category. If the virus continues to spread undetected, it may progress to the next phase.

Critical-Mass Infection Phase

Once the virus spread has reached the *critical-mass infection phase*, the infection spread has mushroomed and reached a level of widespread infection that would be difficult to stop. Only a few viruses reach this phase. Today's more prevalent viruses became widespread because they reached a level of critical mass before the antivirus industry provided sufficient protection or the computing community used the antivirus protection.

The total virus spread has reached a point that between 10 to 26 percent of U.S. companies report they have encountered a computer virus on at least one of their personal computers. If an average company has about 50 personal computers, that total equates to roughly 1 in 300 PCs infected once.

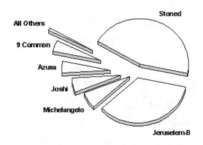

Figure 2-2 Comparison of virus spread in the United States

A few widespread viruses account for the bulk of the virus encounter reports. If you should ever encounter a virus, it will most likely be one of these five. Virus encounter surveys, and virus fighters we interviewed, all agree on the most widely spread viruses. The percentage of the spread of infection varies, but the ranking order is well accepted. (High and low percentages of virus spread are given so that you can see the range of infection spread reported by differing sources.)

Stoned (40%–60%): A boot-sector virus that randomly displays Your PC is now stoned when your computer is booted.

Jerusalem-B (30%–45%): The only widespread program-infector virus, Jerusalem is also commonly know as the Friday the 13th, because that's the day the virus *deletes* programs rather than *infecting* them.

Michelangelo (5%–16%): The infamous boot-sector virus that spreads without any obvious symptoms, until March 6 when it celebrates the artist's birthday by overwriting the infected hard disk.

Joshi (4%–8%): On January 5, this boot-sector virus displays Happy Birthday Joshi. The virus waits until the user answers back **Happy Birthday Joshi**, and then returns control to the interrupted program.

Azusa (3%–7%): Also known as the Hong Kong virus, the Azusa virus is another boot-sector virus. It disables the communication ports and the printer ports every 32nd time the computer is operated.

The following nine other common viruses account for less than 5 percent of the virus spread in the U.S. In relation to the top five, their numbers are so statistically small that it is difficult to obtain reliable data concerning the exact percentage of virus infection.

Brain: Also known as the Pakistani Brain, this boot-sector virus significantly slows down the boot process and changes an infected disk's volume label to: (c) Brain.

Cascade: Alias *Falling Letters*, this .COM program infector causes the characters on the screen to fall and collect at the bottom, but only during the months of fall.

Dark Avenger: The virus program infector will slowly write over single sectors, gradually corrupting programs and data.

Dir-2: This stealth virus infects not programs or boot sectors, but the directory structure. It causes lost clusters, but the greatest damage is done when CHKDSK /F attempts to repair the damage, creating cross-linked clusters instead.

Disk Killer: This boot-sector virus waits 48 hours, and then effectively scrambles your disk.

Empire: Also known as the Evil Empire-B, this boot-sector virus sometimes displays the message PC♥AT LIVE F♥R U♥VE ♥♥ when booting.

Ping Pong (Italian-A): This virus randomly turns your computer into a playerless game of Pong. Once activated, the only way to turn off the boot-sector virus's bouncing ball is to reboot.

Music Bug: When booting from a disk infected with this boot-sector virus, the computer may "click" or play music through the PC speaker.

Sunday: This program infector activates on any Sunday, and displays the message: Today is Sunday! Why do you work so hard? All work and no play makes you a dull boy! Come on! Let's go out and have some fun! The Sunday virus also causes File Allocation Table problems.

All the other viruses combined represent less than 1 percent of the virus infect spread in the United States.

Effect Phase

Viruses usually don't activate their most dramatic symptoms immediately but wait for a certain trigger date or certain event. This delay gives the virus time to replicate while remaining hidden. The effect is most dramatic when the virus is triggered on a specific date. The whole world experiences the effect simultaneously, as in the case of the March 6 Michelangelo virus trigger date.

Once the virus has made itself known and alerted computer users to its presence, the virus is usually removed from the system. Several viruses self-destruct while damaging the host software. Other viruses that do not self-destruct are so random in their effect that the *effect phase* never causes a widespread identification of the virus. Following are some typical effect triggers:

- Completely random. When programs infected with the Ambulance Car virus are executed, about 1 percent of the time a graphic ambulance moves across the bottom of the screen with an audible siren.

- Several viruses are date activated. See Appendix B for a complete list of the virus activation dates.

- The boot count or number of times the computer is started. This is also an activation trigger, as in the case of the Telecom virus that destroys all software on the hard disk on its 400th boot.

- Time since boot. The Jerusalem virus's black box appears after the virus has been live for 30 minutes.

- Keystroke count. Once the Fingers virus is live in memory, it counts your keystrokes and activates when the count hits 400.

All viruses alter software, and most operate as ill-behaved memory-resident programs. Even seemingly benign viruses present some level of risk to your computer system's integrity. As we saw in the last chapter, there are other viruses that are intended to be dangerous. Following are types of damage viruses are known to do:

- Unpartition the hard disk by corrupting the disk's partition table

- Reformat the hard disk

- Delete files

- Corrupt files

- Alter data files

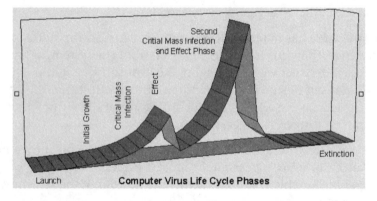

Figure 2-3 Sample life cycle of a typical computer virus

The graph illustrates the life of a virus, showing how the virus spreads completely unchecked through two destructive effect trigger dates. In this example, the computing community takes protective measures after the second trigger date, and then the virus is eliminated.

Real life is often more muddled than this straightforward example. Alerts will be posted before the effect date. As with the Michelangelo virus, preventive warnings can be effective before the trigger date.

The End of the Virus Life Cycle

Fortunately, the majority of viruses reach a premature end as antivirus software halts their growth before they obtain the critical-mass required to become widespread. Other viruses reach their end as the result of hundreds of users experiencing problems and fighting the viruses the hard way.

A virus is considered *endangered* if it becomes increasingly uncommon, or due to a bug or design flaw will probably never become common. *Extinct* viruses are those which once were common, but no report of an infection has been made for over a year.

Program-Infecting Virus Reproductive Cycle

Program-infector viruses infect program files. To see exactly how the program infection takes place, let's walk through a typical computer virus reproductive cycle:

1. As the reproductive cycle begins, we'll assume the virus is already attached to a program (HOST1.COM).

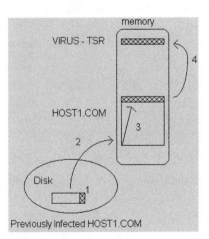

Figure 2-4 A virus loading as TSR

2. HOST1.COM is executed.

3. The virus within HOST1.COM is executed as the first module of HOST1.COM.

4. The virus loads itself into memory as a memory-resident or TSR (Terminate and Stay Resident) program.

Technically, the virus will usually hook an interrupt (often Interrupt 21, the DOS Request Interrupt). MS-DOS uses interrupts to allow programs and routines to respond to activities within the system. Whenever an interrupt is activated, any TSR that has hooked that same interrupt is executed so that it can provide further processing. (This is how any TSR can operate on a "run only as necessary" basis.) By hooking Int 21, the viral code in memory is executed whenever any program executes a DOS request. The virus can then freely watch all DOS file operations.

If the virus loads in any unused free memory (see figure 2.5) or loads in any unused allocated system memory (Lehigh virus example), the virus may be overwritten by DOS or another program as it loads. The virus may still be able to infect the loading program because the virus will be able to act on the "Open File" interrupt before the file overwrites the virus.

Depending on where and how the virus loads in memory, you may be able to find the live virus in memory manually. The viral TSRTSR may be reported by DOS's MEM /C, Norton Utilities' SYSINFO, or Quarterdeck's Manifest. Because a viral TSR is often an ill-behaved program and may not follow the normal TSR rules, it is possible that one of these utilities will find the virus while the other two will miss the viral TSR.

The viral TSR will bear the name of the infected program that the virus used to become live in memory. For example, if MEM.COM was infected with the Fellowship virus, the Fellowship TSR would be reported as MEM.COM, a 1K program. Since MEM.COM does not load, if MEM.COM is reported as a TSR it's a dead giveaway of viral activity.

More confusing, however, is if the infected program normally loads memory resident, as in the case of MOUSE.COM. If it became infected with the Jerusalem virus, the MEM /C report would show two

Mouse TSR programs. The first would be the normal 11K mouse driver. The second Mouse TSR is the Jerusalem virus that loads with the execution of MOUSE.COM as a TSR.

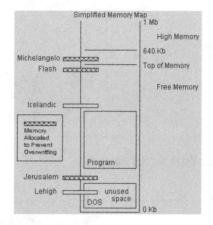

Figure 2-5 Viral TSR locations in memory

Without presenting a complete course in PC memory management, following are some basics to help you understand where viruses load.

Base memory (sometimes called conventional memory) is the first 640Kb of RAM that DOS uses to load system and application programs. The actual "cap" on base memory is called *Top of Memory* by DOS. The memory areas above 640Kb and to 1024Kb contain various system ROM functions. Today's memory managers (DOS 5.0 HIMEM.SYS, Qualitas 386Max, Quarterdeck QEMM) load TSRs in unused portions of high memory to leave more base memory available for application programs.

If the virus is loaded outside normal DOS memory (above Top of Memory), such as Michelangelo, the virus steals conventional memory from DOS. This results in the simple equation of amount of memory usable by DOS decreased by the size of the viral TSR. *Total Available Memory* is easily reported by DOS's MEM, CHKDSK commands, Norton Utilities' SYSINFO, or Quarterdeck's Manifest.

5. HOST1.COM is executed and completed as usual. However, the virus is still loaded in computer memory as a TSR even after the program HOST1.COM is exited.

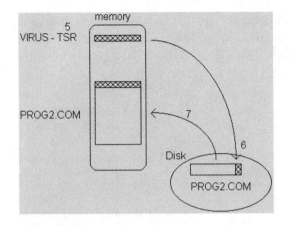

Figure 2-6 A virus infecting a second program

Once the virus is live in memory it may begin to display the following symptoms:

- System slowdown

- Corruption of system or files

- Messages, displayed or hidden in the virus. Some messages may be coded or encrypted.

- Graphics on the screen

- File date or time change

- System reboots

- Music

- Sound effects

- Some elusive viruses won't present any symptoms at all

6. The user runs a second program (PROG2.COM). As DOS loads PROG2.COM into memory to begin execution, the virus intercepts the DOS file open request. The virus then infects PROG2.COM on the disk. The viral code is added to the end of PROG2.COM, and the beginning program code in PROG2.COM is altered so that the virus will be executed before the bulk of PROG2.COM loads into memory.

Some viruses limit themselves to only specific types of programs while others are generic infectors that infect just about any program. The actual infection can take place in the following ways:

- Some viruses attach themselves to the end of the infected program, permitting the infected program to operate normally.

- Less sophisticated viruses overwrite a part of the infected file, clobbering the infected file's programming code and making the program unusable.

- Program infecting stealth viruses will search for holes or unused portions of the program to infect. This action allows the virus to hide within the program.

7. Later, the user runs PROG3.COM and PROG4.COM. They are both infected in the same manner PROG2 was infected.

8. During the next computing session, if HOST1.COM, PROG2.COM, PROG3.COM, or PROG4.COM is re-executed, the virus reproduction cycle will be repeated again and again; any new programs that are run will become infected.

Boot-Sector Viruses

Four of the five most widely spread viruses are *boot-sector* viruses. These viruses attach themselves to the executable portion of the disk or diskette. This design gives them the following advantages over program-infecting viruses:

- Data diskettes are shared more often than programs. Computer users generally believe that BBSes and infected programs spread viruses. Many are shocked to learn that a blank diskette is a common carrier.

- The boot-sector virus's simpler reproductive method does not depend on programs being executed. Once a computer is infected with a boot-sector virus, the virus is constantly live.

- The boot sector is well documented and easily infected without any strange side effects.

To understand how a boot sector virus operates, it's important to understand the boot sequence.

The Normal Boot Process

The boot process happens so fast on most computers that it is easy for you to be unaware of the many steps involved in booting an MS-DOS computer. The key player is the ROM-BIOS (Read Only Memory - Basic Input Output System), which consists of the two ROM chips on your computer system board.

1. Turn on your machine.

2. The video card ROM-BIOS boots and often displays a nice color message on the top line of the monitor screen. Next, any other special ROM-BIOS additions are executed (ESDI controllers or SCSI host adapters).

3. The system board's ROM-BIOS chip executes the POST (Power On Self Test) test. This internal test counts memory and checks other attached devices. Any problems detected by POST are usually displayed using the original IBM PC error numbering standard (i.e., POST will display 1704 for a hard disk controller error).

4. Next, the ROM-BIOS attempts to load DOS from a diskette in the A: drive. The first sector of every diskette is the boot sector. If the diskette is a bootable diskette, the boot sector holds a small program that locates and runs DOS.

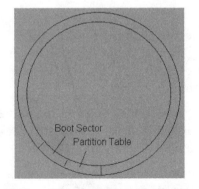

Figure 2-7 The partition table and boot sector of the hard disk

5. If the diskette in the A: drive is simply a data diskette and not bootable, the boot sector contains a small program that displays the message Non-System disk or disk-error and waits for a keystroke before executing a warm boot to re-attempt the boot process again. That's why different diskettes can display a different message when left in the A: drive. For example, diskettes formatted with Norton's "Safe Format" display a very different error message.

NOTE: Using Norton Utilities, it is possible to edit the message in the boot sector program to display any message you prefer, such as "ABC Corp. Property." One infamous prank was to edit the boot sector message to display 1704: Hard Disk Failure thus eliciting a perfectly erroneous error message.

6. If there is no diskette in the A: drive, the ROM-BIOS continues with the boot attempt by looking at the first sector (or the partition table) of hard disk 0 (the first hard disk listed in your CMOS setup), commonly referred to as *C:*. This sector contains information about which disk partition is active (bootable) and where the partition starts on the disk.

7. The ROM-BIOS now executes the first sector of the active partition, usually the second physical sector of your hard drive. This sector, known as the *boot sector*, contains a small executable program that launches DOS (specifically, the two hidden system files—MSDOS.SYS and IO.SYS).

8. DOS finally loads and configures itself automatically, according to your commands in the file CONFIG.SYS. Once DOS is up and running, it executes COMMAND.COM which in turn executes AUTOEXEC.BAT. If AUTOEXEC.BAT is not found, COMMAND.COM will display a message and ask you for the current date and time.

Reproductive Cycle

The boot-sector virus's reproduction is designed to take advantage of how the ROM-BIOS searches for and executes DOS. As we begin the virus's reproductive cycle, we'll assume a diskette is infected and the computer is turned off.

1. The diskette is in the A: drive. Perhaps during your last computing session, you copied files from the diskette and left the diskette in the drive accidentally.

2. The computer is now turned on. The ROM-BIOS looks for a bootable diskette in the A: drive and prepares to execute the diskette's boot sector.

3. When ROM-BIOS executes the diskette's boot sector, the boot-sector virus is really the program that is executed. Once running, the virus quickly checks for the presence of a hard disk and infects either the hard disk partition table or the active partition's boot sector.

The boot sector contains a significant amount of empty space the virus can use. Alternately, the virus can completely move the original partition table or boot sector to another sector, freeing sectors 1 and 2 for the virus to infect. The sector now holding the moved original data is often marked as a bad sector so that it will not be overwritten by subsequent file copies or save commands.

4. Back at the infected diskette in drive A:, the virus now runs the original diskette's boot sector. This example uses a data diskette so that the boot-sector program displays the following message:

```
Non-System disk or disk error

Replace and press any key when ready
```

Your computer is now infected with a boot sector virus. The infection process happened so that, unless you were watching for a different sequence of disk reads and writes during the boot process, you would not notice the infection taking place.

5. In response to the `Non-system disk...` message, you remove the diskette and reboot your machine. This time the virus is loaded from the hard drive and becomes memory resident before DOS is loaded.

6. A program infecting virus does not become live until an infected program is executed. A boot-sector virus is always live on an infected computer as long as the computer is booted from the hard disk. While live, the boot-sector virus watches the diskette drives and infects every diskette the DOS has access to during

reads and writes. Even a simple DIR A: will infect the diskette. An office that uses several diskettes to pass data will quickly fester with the virus infection as nearly every diskette becomes infected.

Stealth Viruses

Stealth viruses can be either program infectors or boot-sector viruses—the virus's advanced methods of eluding detection are what make it a stealth. The term *stealth virus* first appeared in 1990 in research labs developing advanced viruses to test antivirus software for the military.

The name "stealth virus" sounds scarier than it is. Stealth virus methods are an advance (?) in viral technology; however, even stealth viruses have limitations. They must be executed to load into memory and must make a modification to a file to infect a program. Norton AntiVirus detects stealth viruses.

Boot Survivors

As the name implies, *boot survivors* are not affected by a warm boot (Ctrl+Alt+Del). The Alameda virus uses the warm boot as its primary method of reproducing. This is why it's important to completely power off the computer when fighting a virus.

Accelerated Infectors

Most viruses infect programs only as the programs are executed. Accelerated infectors don't wait for a program to be executed before infecting it.

Some *accelerated infectors* (called *fast infectors*) infect program files during a *file open* rather than a *file load*. A file open happens any time the file is read from the disk (i.e., copying or viewing a file). In the worst case scenario, an unknown accelerated-infector virus that is live in memory could infect every program as it is read (scanned) by an antivirus scanner.

Other accelerated infectors will seek out a program and infect it. The *Devil's Dance* virus (one of the nastier viruses) will infect every .COM file it can find as soon as the virus loads into memory.

Dissimulators

Dissimulator viruses (from the Latin *Dissimulatus*, meaning to hide under a false appearance) camouflage their infection. The TSR portion of the virus suspends any attempt to view the file or report on the file size and supplies false information to the requesting program. This false information makes it appear as if the file is not infected. For example, a DIR of a program infected with a dissimulator virus will report the original size of the file as the display would be without the infection.

Disinfectors

The term *disinfector* seems to be a double negative, but it is common for criminal activity to be temporarily hidden as a police car slowly cruises past. In the same way, the TSR portion of a disinfector virus, like Frodo 4096, will actually remove the virus infection from the program file while the file is being scanned by an antivirus program! The virus then reinfects the program after the disk read.

The Frodo virus may sound menacing, but the virus can only disinfect if the virus is actually live in memory. Rebooting with a clean DOS diskette before scanning eliminates the "stealth" from these viruses.

Polymorphic Infectors

Poly, meaning many, and *morphic,* meaning forms, these viruses self-encrypt to make it harder for a virus scanner to detect the virus. This encryption key changes every time the virus is executed. The *Dark Avenger's Mutation Engine (DAME)* is an encryption method used to develop polymorphic viruses. At least two viruses use the DAME: the Pouge Mahone and the Sara viruses.

Norton AntiVirus, Version 2.5, added the capability to detect any virus created with the Mutation Engine.

Multipartite Infectors

These viruses divide and conquer. A *multipartite* (literally "in many parts") *virus* (also known as a "spawning" or "companion file" virus) writes only one copy of the virus to the disk (often an unused portion of the disk, perhaps marking the sector "bad" so that it won't be scanned). Every infected program merely points to or executes the same single copy of the virus code. Infected programs or boot sectors only need to have had one command altered to execute the virus that is hiding elsewhere on the disk. The complete multipartite virus is in two places—the launch code in the infected programs and a separate companion portion of the virus that contains the bulk of the virus code.

This division gives the multipartite stealth virus two significant advantages—it only makes a minuscule change to the infected file and it only needs to hide or protect one copy of the virus. AIDS II and Telecom-2 are both multipartite viruses.

Dir-2

The *Dir-2* virus (also aptly known as the *Creeping Death* virus) is a multipartite accelerated-infecting dissimulator polymorphic virus that is still a threat after booting from a clean DOS diskette. It infects a program without altering the program's file. Instead, the Dir-2 virus alters the File Allocation Table (FAT) so that the virus is executed rather than the program you wanted to run. Once in memory, the Dir-2 spreads very rapidly. Because the FAT is infected, the virus can be replicated by merely copying an infected program file. (The COPY command would be redirected and would copy the virus companion file with the intended program file.) The FAT alteration will cause DOS's CHKDSK to report several lost clusters. Executing CHKDSK /F will result in numerous cross-linked files.

Norton AntiVirus will detect the Dir-2 "Creeping Death" virus. If you encounter Dir-2, stop and call Norton Technical Support at (310) 453-4600 for assistance in removing this virus.

With new viruses constantly being reported, "Computer Virology" becomes a changing science. As viruses evolve, new terms and methods will be used.

Anatomy of the Stoned Virus

A non-stealth boot-sector virus, the *Stoned* virus is easy to detect and remove but is the world's most common virus. As such, it also has a great number of variations and aliases: Donald Duck, Hawaii, Marijuana, New Zealand, Rostov, San Diego, Sex Revolution, Smithsonian, Stoned II, and Deunis. It was discovered in Wellington, New Zealand, in February of 1988.

```
Your PC is now stoned!
```

Symptoms

Besides replicating and displaying its message, Stoned usually causes no damage to the system (some versions may cause RLL disk controllers to hang). The early versions of Stoned would infect only 360Kb diskettes, but the newer, widespread versions infect hard disks and 1.2Mb diskettes.

Randomly (about 1 time in 8) the virus will display a message when the computer is booted. While there are many variations in the message, they all share a common theme of being pro-marijuana, such as `Your PC is now stoned!`.

Some of the more recent variations will beep to make sure you notice the message.

How Stoned Works

If a computer is booted from a Stoned-infected diskette, the virus will activate and infect the hard disk. When it infects the hard disk,

Stoned will copy (or relocate) your original boot sector to track 0, head 0, sector 0.

The `Non-system disk...` message then appears from the diskette's original boot sector.

When you reboot from the hard disk, the virus will load into memory (at Top of Memory) and hook interrupt 12.

You can manually find the Stoned virus by viewing the boot sector with Norton Disk Editor. Choose the partition table as the object, and then choose View as Text. Because of the way Stoned loaded into memory, DOS MEM and CHKDSK will report 2K less than normal of Total Memory Available.

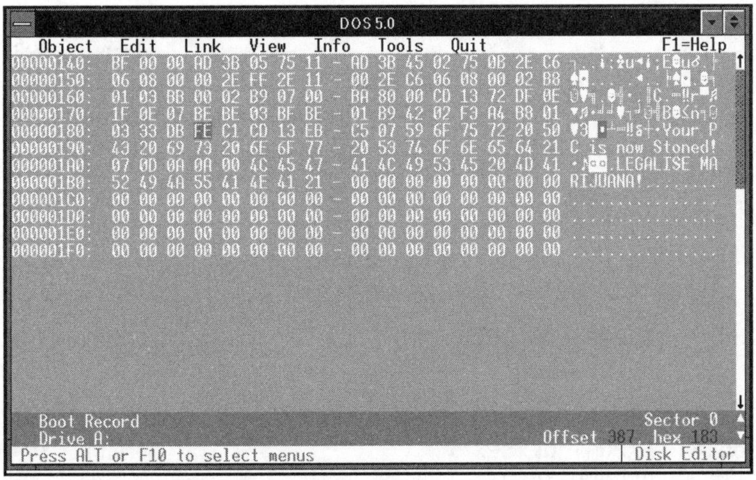

Figure 2-8 Norton DISKEDIT showing the Stoned virus infecting the boot sector

Stoned Virus Strains

The original diskette-only infector is extinct, and all known variants of this virus are capable of infecting the hard disk partition table as well as damaging directory or FAT information. Most variants of this virus have only minor modifications, usually in what the message is that the virus may display on-screen.

Stoned Strain	Randomly displayed during boot	Hidden internal message	Comment
Stoned-A	Your computer is now stoned.	Legalize Marijuana	Does not infect hard disks
Stoned-B	Your computer is now stoned.	Legalize Marijuana	RLL controller changes
Deunis	no display	udEUNaS ABRASa TU cPU (c)IMAN4	from Spain July 91
PS-Stoned	no display	none	New Brunswick, Canada, February 1992, hides on disk— difficult to detect
Rostov	no display	Non System Disk... Replace and strike	Dececember 1990
Sex Revolution v1.1	EXPORT OF SEX REVOLUTION ver. 1.1		December 1990
Sex Revolution v2.0	EXPORT OF SEX REVOLUTION ver. 2.0		December 1990
Stoned-C	no display	no message	
Stoned-D	no display		Now infects high-density diskettes
Stoned-E	Your PC is now Stoned.	LEGALISE MARIJUANA	Now beeps with message
Stoned-F	Twoj PC jest teraz be!	LEGALISE MARIJUANA?	Beeps

Stoned Strain	Randomly displayed during boot	Hidden internal message	Comment
Stoned II	Your PC is now Stoned! Version 2 \<or\> Donald Duck is a lie.		
Stoned-NSD	Non SYStEM dISc	LEGALISE4-MARIJUANA	Discovered east U.S., October 1991
Stoned-NZ	YOUR PC IS NOW STONED!		Potentially destroys partition table, discovered in New Zealand, October, 1991

Anatomy of the Jerusalem Virus

Of the top five viruses, only the *Jerusalem* virus is a program-infector virus. The Jerusalem is by far the most prolific of the program infecting viruses. It has been altered numerous times and its code has been the tutor for many virus writers. Technically, according to Patricia Hoffman's Virus Summary classifications, Jerusalem-B is a Memory Resident Generic File Infector, meaning that it loads into memory as a TSR and then infects both .COM and .EXE files when they are executed.

The Story behind the Virus

The Jerusalem virus was originally written in Italy and is a modification of the Suriv 3 virus. Jerusalem was released in Israel in the fall of 1987 as a terrorist weapon. The plan was for the virus to spread until Friday, May 13, 1988, when the virus would cause widespread software destruction throughout Israel on the 40th anniversary of the end of the Palestine State.

A bug in Jerusalem causes it to reinfect .COM files many times over until some programs will no longer load into memory. This error alerted Israeli computer scientists at the Hebrew University as early as

October, 1987. They then wrote an antivirus program that detected and removed the virus. While planned to activate on Friday, May 13, 1988, the virus would also have activated earlier, on Friday, November 13, 1987.

Symptoms

The Jerusalem virus has many symptoms, ranging from system slowdown to destroying programs. Following is a complete list of symptoms for Jerusalem-B (the most common strain):

- When an infected program is executed, Jerusalem will load into memory as a memory-resident program (TSR). The viral TSR is 1709 bytes in size and has the name of the infected host program. The TSR virus will hook interrupts 08 (Timer Tick) and 21 (MS-DOS Request /function dispatcher).

- Using interrupt 08 (Timer Tick), the Jerusalem virus will do two things after being live (or memory resident) for 30 minutes. First, Jerusalem will slow the system down by a factor of 10, and second, a "black window" or "black box" will appear on the lower left side of the screen. When the screen scrolls the black box will also scroll.

- Once the virus is live in memory, it will infect .COM, .EXE, .SYS, .BIN, .PIF, and some overlay files when those files are executed. A bug in the Jerusalem virus will cause it to reinfect .EXE files multiple times. The Jerusalem virus will not infect COMMAND.COM.

- An infected file will contain the character string "sUMsDos" or a variation depending on the Jerusalem strain. The Jerusalem Strains chart details the message and the imbedded character string for each viral strain, and the most deadly symptom.

- Any program you might attempt to run on occurrences of Friday the 13th will be destroyed. Some deleted programs can be repaired with Norton UnErase, depending on which Jerusalem strain caused the damage. Otherwise, you must restore from a backup or completely reinstall the program. It has been reported in other books about viruses that data files are at risk from Jerusalem virus attacks. Our testing shows that data files are not affected.

- The infamous Jerusalem "Black Box" and system slow down. This machine measured 9.4 on the Norton SI scale before the infection.

How Jerusalem Works

The file *JER-B.COM* was programmed to do nothing more than display the message `Hello World!`, and then exit. The file was infected with Jerusalem-B for test purposes.

In the following walk through a Jerusalem-B infection we will do the following:

- Check the initial size of MEM.EXE.

- Display conventional memory as it exists before the infection using the DOS 5.0 MEM /C command.

- Execute JER-B.COM, infecting the computer with Jerusalem-B. At this point, Jerusalem-B loads into memory as a TSR and is considered a live virus.

- Run the DOS memory command to see the virus loaded as a memory-resident program (TSR).

- Recheck the size of MEM.EXE (it has grown by 1814 bytes). Since the DOS 5.0 memory command is an .EXE file, Jerusalem will reinfect every time MEM.EXE is executed.

```
C:\VIRUSES>DIR \DOS\MEM.EXE

Volume in Drive C is Virus Test

Volume Serial Number is 521B-14E9

Directory of C:\DOS


MEM      EXE    39818 04-09-91      5:00a
   1 file(s)     43440 bytes
          16877568 bytes free


C:\VIRUSES>MEM /C


Conventional Memory :
```

```
Name                Size in Decimal         Size in Hex

MSDOS               18832   (18.4K)          4990

HIMEM                2896   ( 2.8K)          B50

SETVER                432   ( 0.4K)          1B0

ANSI                 4192   ( 4.1K)          1060

COMMAND              3392   ( 3.3K)          D40

FREE                   64   ( 0.1K)          40

FREE               625328  (610.7K)          98AB0


Total FREE :       625392   (610.7K)


Total bytes available to programs :  625392   (610.7K)

Largest executable program size :    625072   (610.4K)


1048576 bytes total contiguous extended memory

        0 bytes available contiguous extended
        memory

  983040 bytes available XMS memory

      MS-DOS resident in High Memory Area


C:\VIRUSES>JER-B

Hello World!


C:\VIRUSES>MEM /C


Conventional Memory :


Name                Size in Decimal         Size in Hex

MSDOS               18832  ( 18.4K)          4990

HIMEM                2896  ( 2.8K)           B50
```

```
SETVER          432   ( 0.4K)        1B0

ANSI           4192   ( 4.1K)        1060

COMMAND        3392   ( 3.3K)        D40

JER-B          1792   ( 1.8K)        700

FREE             64   ( 0.1K)        40

FREE            240   ( 0.2K)        F0

FREE         623264   (608.7K)       982A0


Total FREE :   623568    (609.0K)


Total bytes available to programs :   623568   (609.0K)

Largest executable program size :     623264   (608.7K)


1048576 bytes total contiguous extended memory

        0 bytes available contiguous extended
        memory

  983040 bytes available XMS memory

      MS-DOS resident in High Memory Area


C:\VIRUSES>DIR \DOS\MEM.EXE


Volume in Drive C is Virus Test

Volume Serial Number is 521B-14E9

Directory of C:\DOS


MEM    EXE    41632 04-09-91  5:00a

    1 file(s)   43440 bytes

            16877568 bytes free


C:\VIRUSES>
```

Using Norton's DISKEDIT, both programs (JER-B.COM and the Jerusalem-B Virus in memory) contained the strings "sUMsDos" and "COMMAND.COM." MEM.EXE and DISKEDIT.EXE also contained the telltale messages.

Norton DiskEdit - Jerusalem-B infection

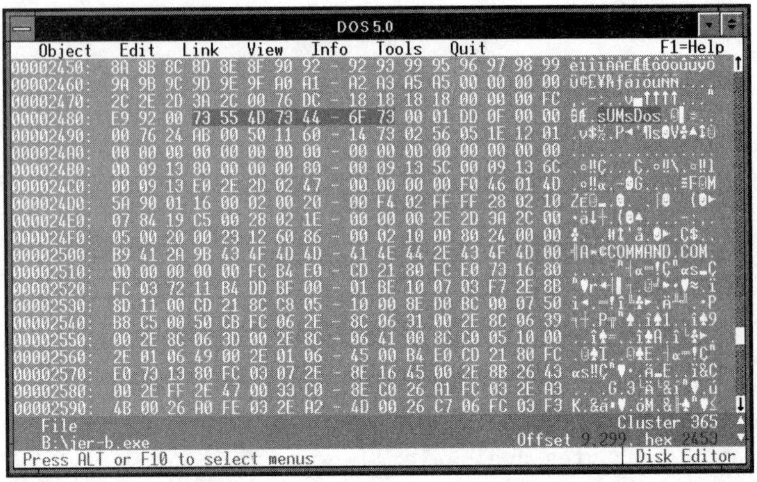

Figure 2-9 Norton DiskEdit view of the Jerusalem-B virus infection of MEM.COM

Norton SysInfo - Memory TSR report

We just infected several programs with the Jerusalem virus. Now, to test Jerusalem's destructive capability, the system date is set to Friday, March 13, 1992, and the test PC is rebooted so that Jerusalem-B recognizes the new date.

```
C:\VIRUSES>Date

Current date is Thu 03-16-1992

Enter new date (mm-dd-yy): 03-13-92

C:\VIRUSES>
```

The computer is physically powered off and on. The Jerusalem virus is loaded into memory again. This time when MEM.EXE is executed,

Jerusalem deletes MEM.COM and displays the message that MEM cannot be run.

```
C:\>CD\Viruses

C:\VIRUSES>JER-B

Hello World!

C:\VIRUSES>MEM /C

Cannot execute C:\VIRUS\MEM.EXE
```

Jerusalem Strains

The Jerusalem was one of the first widely spread viruses. It has gotten into the hands of many rogue programmers. The result is a huge variety of strains from all over the globe.

Virus	Date	Origin	String	Del Date	Black Box	Slow Down	Other
Jer A	Jan. 91		sUMsDos	Fri 13			
Jer B		Italy	sUMsDos	Fri 13			wide-spread
A-204		Delft, Netherlands	*A-204*	Fri 13	30 min	30 min	size 2288
Anarkia		Spain	ANARKIA	Tues 13	no	greater	
Anarkia-B		Spain	ANARKIA	Oct. 12	no	greater	
Antiviru	Jan. 92	unknown	COMMAND.COM ANTIVIRU	Fri 13	30 min	30 min	
Apocalypse	May 91	Italy	COMMAND.COM Apocalypse!!! C.J**	n/a	30 min	no	
Captain Trips	Mar. 91	U.S.	Captain Trips X	no	no	no	
Captain Trips 2	Mar. 91	U.S.	Captain Trips X	no	no	no	altered to avoid detection
Get Password 1	'91	Europe		no	no	no	Novell specific but buggy

Virus	Date	Origin	String	Del Date	Black Box	Slow Down	Other
Jan. 25th			00 in hex	Jan. 25			
Jan. 25th - B							slight code changes
Jer-C	'88	Israel		Fri 13	30 min	no	
Jer-D	Fri 13			Fri 13 after 1990			
Jer-CD		Washing-ton, DC	00 hex	30 min	30 min	30%	no damage
Jer-E	Fri 13			after 1992			
Jer-PLO			sU?sDos	second half of year		30 min	replicate during first half of year
JVT1			sUMsDns	Tues 1	30 min	30 min	Vertical box with 2 charac-ters in upper left of screen.
JVT1-B	Jan. 92		sUMsDns	Tues 1	30 min	30 min	Slight modified version of JVT1
Mendoza		Argentina	sUMsDos			10%	30 min chance during second half of year
Messina	Nov. 91	Messina		Fri 13	30 min	30 min	
Nemisis	Nov. 91		UM Do NEMESIS.COM NOKEY	Fri 13	30 min	30 min	

Virus	Date	Origin	String	Del Date	Black Box	Slow Down	Other
New Jer	Oct. 89	Netherlands	sUMsDos	Fri 13	30 min	30 min	
Pay Day	Nov. 89	Netherlands	sUMsDos	all Fri except 13	30 min	30 min	
Park ESS .COM	Oct. 90	Happy Camp California	PARK ESS	30 min	30 min	20%	Will infect COMMAND
Phenome	May 91	Italy	MsDos PHENOME.COM	all Sat			Program will not execute, but not destroyed.
Puerto	June 90	Puerto Rico	sUMsDos	10% chance during second half of year			30 min
Skism	Jan. 92	Canada	KISM	Fri after the 15th	30 min	30 min	
Skism-1	Dec. 90	New York	SKISM-1	Fri after the 15th	30 min	30 min	
Spanish-JB							
Jerusalem E2							
Jerusalem F				Fri 13	30 min		
Swiss 1813		Spain		Fri 13			

Anatomy of the Michelangelo Virus

No description of well-known viruses would be complete without a detailed account of the Michelangelo virus. The Michelangelo story was covered in the last chapter. Here we'll take a more technical look at this boot-sector virus.

How It Spreads

To prep the computer for a controlled Michelangelo infection, first we boot from a clean DOS diskette and scan the hard disk with

Norton AntiVirus's Virus Clinic to ensure the disk is virus-free. Next, Norton Disk Doctor is run to check the integrity of the disk. The last step in preparation of the Michelangelo infection is to save snapshots of the partition table and boot records and CMOS values with Norton Rescue. Now we're ready to walk through an encounter with the virus that made the *Wall Street Journal*.

With the computer on and Norton AntiVirus's Comprehensive Scan running, a Michelangelo-infected diskette is placed in the A: drive and the machine is rebooted (press Ctrl+Alt+Del). Norton AntiVirus's Virus Intercept scans the diskette for any boot-sector viruses and warns that the diskette contains the Michelangelo virus.

Disregarding Virus Intercept's warnings, we reboot the computer from the infected diskette in the A: drive. The PC activates the diskette drives and the hard disk as it normally does. But then it activates the A: drive once more and the hard disk light blinks as Michelangelo infects the hard disk. There is no perceptible delay to indicate the virus had traveled from the floppy to the hard disk. If we weren't closely watching the hard disk light for the infection, we might have missed it.

The following message appeared:

```
Non-System disk or disk error - Replace and press any
key when ready.
```

The infected diskette was removed from the diskette drive and returned to the virus library. I pressed a key and the machine appeared to boot normally off the hard drive. The DOS MEM command, however, reported total conventional memory as 653,312 or 2K less than the 655,360 DOS normally reports.

Removing Mike

The machine is rebooted again, this time from a clean DOS 5.0 diskette. Norton AntiVirus's Virus Clinic locates the Michelangelo virus on drive C: and removes it. Rebooting from C: and running DOS MEM confirmed that the virus was no longer present.

NOTE: On some computers, depending on the DOS version and computer manufacturer, it is possible to remove a boot-sector virus with the undocumented command FDISK /MBR. During our testing we found that this method worked more than half of the time.

The Damage

We infected the hard disk again with Michelangelo. This time, rather than removing the infection, we let it run its course and destroy the hard disk's partitioning.

But first, we tested a rumor. During the Michelangelo media coverage in March 1992, it was reported that Michelangelo might activate on any date on or after March 6, Michelangelo's actual birthday.

We changed the CMOS date to March 7, 1992, and then rebooted. Other than the same lack of 2K conventional memory, everything still appeared to operate normally.

Now for the March 6 test. We again changed the CMOS date, this time to March 6, 1992.

The computer was rebooted. The diskette light was activated as usual, but the hard disk light remained turned on, as if it were stuck. We waited ten minutes and Michelangelo continued to write to the hard disk. If fact, there is a bug in Michelangelo that causes it to loop indefinitely, writing to the hard disk.

To assess the damage, we attempted to reboot from the C: drive and the following message appeared:

```
DRIVE NOT READY - insert boot diskette in A: Press any
key when ready.
```

We rebooted from a clean DOS diskette and attempted to move to the C: drive. It appeared as if there were no C: drive, and the following message appeared:

```
A:>C:

Invalid Drive Specification

A:
```

In an attempt to recover from the damage, we used Norton AntiVirus Rescue to restore the corrupted boot record areas from the rescue data. Rescue also set the CMOS date back from 3-6-92. Running Virus Clinic, it could no longer locate Michelangelo on the hard disk.

The C: drive seemed to be restored, but the program and data on the disk were also overwritten by the virus. A directory of C: appeared normal; however, when we attempted to run a program from C:, the following error appeared:

```
Sector not found reading drive C:
Abort, Retry, Ignore, Fail?
```

The only way to make the computer usable is to repartition and reformat the hard disk. The programs must be reinstalled or restored from a backup. Data files, of course, must also be restored from a backup.

Fighting the Good Fight

The spread of viruses is much like a circle. An infected file (for example A.EXE) is executed (disk read). The virus loads into memory. The virus watches other disk activity and infects another executable file, B.EXE (disk write). Later, B.EXE is executed and the cycle begins again. The question for every antivirus program development team is "At which point in the virus cycle should Norton AntiVirus detect and stop the virus?"

Consider the differences between a virus while it lies dormant in an infected file and when it becomes "live" as a running program in memory.

- Once a virus is active in memory, it can claim interrupts and can "take over" parts of DOS. Viruses are weaker when they are in a dormant state and only in a file.

- A virus loads into memory with only one disk read. The disk read is executed by DOS and happens in a normal predictable manner. A virus infection, however, happens several times in the life of a virus and is in charge of the disk write. The virus has the opportunity to bypass DOS or attempt to hide its actions.

- A virus in an infected file is potential danger; a virus running in memory is an active enemy that is watching to infect more files and waiting for the "trigger" that tells the unleashed virus to cause damage.

Where To Draw the Line?

For these three reasons, the Norton AntiVirus development team decided to make their "line in the sand" at the point that the virus attempts to go "live" and load into memory. That's why Virus Intercept, the defensive portion of Norton AntiVirus, watches the disk reads, not the disk writes, for a virus.

This *line of defense*—preventing a virus from being read from the disk—may first seem to be like closing the barn door after the horse got out. The disk read defense, however, prevents a virus from becoming "live" in memory from a diskette and infecting a hard disk. By stopping a virus from running in memory, Virus Intercept provides extremely sound protection against viruses.

Summary

Computer viruses, like biological viruses, spread by replicating themselves within their host program (or cell). Computer viruses fall into two broad groups: boot-sector infectors (that spread by the sharing of infected diskettes) and program infectors (that spread by executing infected programs). Stealth viruses can be either boot sector or program infector viruses that use advanced techniques to hide their infection.

Although there are hundreds of virus strains, the bulk of the virus infects boil down to a handful of viruses. The most common virus is the Stoned virus, a boot-sector virus that randomly displays Your PC is Stoned upon booting. Jerusalem is the most widely spread program-infecting virus. This virus deletes programs on any Friday the 13th.

Viruses have inherent weaknesses. Before they become live in memory, a virus is just code on the disk. By taking advantage of viruses' weaknesses, fighting viruses is made easier and safer.

Strategies for Safe Computing

The most important guideline for safe computing—know your computer. You can only tell when your computer is acting strangely if you know how it behaves normally.

You can feel when your car's brakes need adjusting. You can hear when your home's air conditioner is running too long or working too hard because the air filter needs changing. In the same way, you can tell when your system is slowing down and the hard disk needs optimizing or when copying a file to a diskette takes too long.

These guidelines for safe computing even go beyond basic virus protection. The sense of knowing the "inside" and "outside" of personal computing encompasses all aspects of personal computing.

The Inside

Inside your computer are the programs and data, memory and CPUs, drives, and the power supply. It is in this inner circle that safe computing begins. Once the system is clean on the inside, we can look at how to keep it clean from the outside.

Clean Hardware

We used to buy PCs the way we buy cars. The new model would come out and we would buy a whole new car.

The life of a computer used to be about two years, but now the box, power supply, diskette drives, and more will stay for years. Perhaps you'll swap the system board a few times, upgrade to a faster video board, or add another hard drive and keep the machine running much longer. The point is simply that every part of the PC is just an upgradable component. PCs are no longer like cars. There's no need to buy a whole PC just to get a new, faster engine, a new model body, or an air bag. From modern folklore comes the woodsman's ax story:

"Yep, this here ax is the best ax I've ever had. My Papa gave it to me, and my Granddad gave it to him. I've only had to put five new heads 'n' four new handles on it. Good ax."

Taking care of your computer takes on a different meaning if you're planning on keeping the system for a long, long time. So let's look at the computer components with an eye toward longevity.

Power Supply

Every component in the computer depends on the power supply to deliver clean DC current. Any problems with the DC power will shorten the life of the hard drive, system board, or other boards.

Consider upgrading your computer to a higher-quality power supply. There are replacement power supplies that provide DC power that is 20 times cleaner than conventional power supplies.

Mini-Desktop Case

Keep the system clean and off the floor. It is tempting to reclaim some desktop real estate by placing the system on the floor. The problem is that the power supply blows air out of the computer. The negative air pressure in the computer pulls in air and dust through every crack and slot. Open any system that has been on the floor for only a few months and you'll find that the diskette drives, power supply, system board, and everything else are covered with dust. Systems on the desk stay much cleaner than systems on the floor.

The need for the tower systems is less today than a few years ago. The capacity of today's PC components enables you to fit plenty of power in a mini-desktop or mini-tower case. Most small cases allow four or five half-height devices, usually with three external bays and two internal bays.

For example, a mini-desktop could be fully configured and still have an open bay for expansion:

- Dual diskette, 3 1/2-inch and 5 1/4-inch in one device
- Tape backup drive
- CD-ROM drive
- Medium (100-200Mb) hard drive
- Open for hard-drive expansion

Hardware Configuration

Mind your IRQs. *Hardware interrupt (IRQ)* conflicts can cause immediate software/hardware problems, or simply slow performance and cause certain software to behave erratically. Norton Utilities' SysInfo and Norton Desktop's System Info Tool include a display that lists the current interrupt assignments. This can help you identify available interrupts. In the following example, IRQ 2 and IRQ 5 are open for new hardware devices (see figure 3-1).

System Information

File   Summary   Help

Real Mode Software Interrupts

#	INTERRUPT NAME	ADDRESS	OWNER
00	Divide by Zero	0116:108A	DOS System Area
01	Single Step	0070:06F4	DOS System Area
02	Nonmaskable	0A54:0016	DOS System Area
03	Breakpoint	0070:06F4	DOS System Area
04	Overflow	0070:06F4	DOS System Area
05	Print Screen	F000:FF54	BIOS
06	Invalid Opcode	F000:95F2	BIOS
07	Reserved	F000:95F2	BIOS
08	IRQ0 - System Timer	1FCD:0000	WIN386.EXE
09	IRQ1 - Keyboard	1531:0143	TIGACD.EXE
0A	IRQ2	F000:95F2	BIOS
0B	IRQ3 - COM2	0A54:006F	DOS System Area
0C	IRQ4 - COM1	F000:95F2	BIOS
0D	IRQ5	F000:95F2	BIOS
0E	IRQ6 - Diskette	0A54:00B7	DOS System Area
0F	IRQ7 - Printer	0070:06F4	DOS System Area
10	Video	1FD8:000F	WIN386.EXE
11	Equipment Determination	F000:F84D	BIOS
12	Memory Size Determination	F000:F841	BIOS
13	Fixed Disk/Diskette	0C46:168A	SMARTDRV
14	Asynchronous Communication	F000:E739	BIOS
15	System Services	1F8F:0000	WIN386.EXE
16	Keyboard	F000:E82E	BIOS
17	Printer	F000:EFD2	BIOS
18	Resident BASIC	F000:5FF5	BIOS
19	Bootstrap Loader	0C46:1755	SMARTDRV
1A	Real-Time Clock Services	F000:FE6E	BIOS
1B	Keyboard Break	0324:019F	DOS System Area

Figure 3-1 Norton SysInfo reporting interrupts

Get plenty of memory. *RAM* is increasingly inexpensive—use as much as your programs need. Several programs take advantage of expanded memory and run much smoother with extra RAM. A *disk cache* also improves all-around performance. It's amazing how much faster Windows runs when it has enough memory that it doesn't need to swap to the disk.

Operating System

Stay current with the standards around you. If your company uses a particular memory management program, you should support the use of that program. Don't rush to upgrade to every new release; however, it is a good idea to stay as close to the current version as you believe is safe.

Delete DOS's FORMAT.COM and FDISK.EXE so that an ANSI bomb, rogue batch file, or Trojan Horse program can't use DOS's hard disk utilities against you. You still have a copy of FORMAT.COM and FDISK.EXE on your DOS diskettes. Alternately, you could move FORMAT.COM to a different directory that is not in your DOS PATH.

Copy Norton Safe Format (SFORMAT.EXE) to \DOS as NFORMAT.EXE. As with DOS's FORMAT.COM, you are safer if you use a nonstandard name for any format utility.

Avoid using ANSI.SYS and you immediately disable the threat of ANSI bombs, one of the fastest growing types of rogue software. If you must use ANSI, use a safe ANSI.SYS that forgoes the keyboard remapping, or use ANSI.COM from *PC Magazine* that can be loaded and unloaded for specific applications.

Never boot from a diskette unless you are running diagnostics or fighting a virus. Booting from a diskette is the major way that computer viruses spread.

To prevent accidentally booting from a diskette, never leave a diskette in the A: drive. Another tip is to use your least common type of diskette as drive A:. For example, if you primarily use 3 1/2-inch diskettes, make the 5 1/4-inch diskette drive the A: drive to avoid booting from a 3 1/2-inch diskette left in the drive. (To switch your diskette drives, swap the floppy/data cable connection and change the drive designations in the CMOS setup.)

NOTE: Be sure to write-protect your working diskette copies of DOS and other critical utility diskettes.

Current Programs

Try to stay with the current version of your favorite software. It becomes difficult to support older software. You are often needlessly exposing yourself to software bugs and incompatibilities by using older software. Keep in mind that you should test all new software releases and convert to the upgrade only after you have proven to yourself the new software works. For example, if you are upgrading to a new version of your spreadsheet program, install the new version in a separate directory and try it using the spreadsheets you developed. The most critical test that any new software release must pass is accomplishing your tasks on your computer.

Disk Management

Use a good disk-management program. Knowing which programs are where and properly organizing them will reduce the chance of duplicate data files, incompatibilities due to multiple versions, and lost data. Norton Desktop, Norton Commander, Windows' File Manager, and XTreeGold are all very suitable. Programs belong in their own directory under the root directory. The root directory also should be as small as possible.

Try to keep your hard drives at least 20 percent free and regularly run Norton Speed Disk. Disk optimizing not only speeds performance but also helps to reduce errors with disk intensive programs such as MS-Windows or database applications.

Disk caches are becoming commonplace, but not all disk caches are created equal. We recommend you do your own testing with your applications.

Check the amount of memory actually being used by the cache. Testing will let you fine-tune the amount of memory you allocate for the disk cache. You don't want the cache to choke for memory, nor do you want the cache to waste memory. If you use Norton's disk cache, an easy way to test the cache's memory demands under Windows is to run the command NCACHE /REPORT in a DOS window. Paul has found that NCache likes to use 1.6 to 1.8 Mb of RAM with his favorite Windows applications, so he runs NCache with 2Mb of memory.

Catch Problems Early

Use Norton Disk Doctor regularly and avoid DOS's Chkdsk /f like the plague. Depending on the stability of the software you are currently running, you may choose to run the C:\UTILITY\NDD C: /Q command in your AUTOEXEC.BAT to clean up any lost clusters. This command runs Norton Disk Doctor, performing a quick check on drive C:. The quick check runs every NDD test except the Disk scan

Use Norton AntiVirus Virus Intercept to catch any viruses early. In the next section we'll cover Virus Intercept in detail.

Scan all new software with Virus Clinic—even the factory-fresh write-protected commercial software diskettes. There are over 300 documented cases of commercial software shipping with viruses. Virus Clinic is now a Norton Desktop for Windows Desktop Agent. Scanning a diskette is as simple as dragging the files to the Virus Clinic icon and dropping them.

Be Prepared for Problems

Backups are absolutely vital as the best last defense against rogue software, hardware malfunctions, and accidental user errors. Backups require a sound strategy that covers all the bases. We recommend splitting the backup sets into the following three categories:

- The system, DOS, root directory, utilities, Windows
- Your programs
- Your data

You should back up the system whenever you have made a significant change to the system, such as upgrading DOS, Norton Utilities, Windows, or so on. Your programs do not require daily backups. Using two or three backup sets and rotating them should provide sufficient redundancy for system and program backups.

The data backup, on the other hand, requires close regular attention. So that you don't back up every data file every day, use a good incremental/rotation of backup sets. There are as many rotation methods for data backup as there are users who hate to do backups. To find out if the rotation method is "safe computing," ask the following questions:

- Is it simple enough to be followed?

- Is it capable of reconstructing any version of any file from the last two weeks?

- Is it capable of long-term restoration, going back six to twelve months?

The Norton Backup manual has several excellent suggestions to help you develop your backup strategy. Following is a simple suggestion that combines the Grandfather and the Tower of Hanoi rotation methods.

The F-n backup represents full backups, saving every data file on the disk; the I-n or incremental backups are saving only those files that have been modified. Remember, this backup plan is for the data set, so that you need not back up every file, just your data files. Back up the system and program files only as necessary. (Norton Backup excels at dealing with different categories of files and backup sets!) Following is a sample data set backup plan:

Day/Week	Full (F-n)	Incremental (I-n)
Mon	F-1	I-1
Tues		I-2
Wed		I-3
Thurs		I-4
Fri	F-2	
Mon		I-5
Tues		I-6
Wed		I-7
Thru		I-8
Fri	F-3	

Day/Week	Full (F-n)	Incremental (I-n)
Wk 3	F-2	I-1 to I-4
Wk 4	F-4	I-5 to I-8
Wk 5	F-2	I-1 to I-4
Wk 6	F-3	I-5 to I-8
Wk 7	F-2	I-1 to I-4
Wk 8	F-5	I-5 to I-8

Everyone hates to do backups. To make backups a little less painful, back up to tape to eliminate the endless diskette swapping. You also can automate the backup strategy so that you can back up at the end of the day or in the background. (Norton Desktop for Windows Scheduler will automate backup sets and run Norton Backup for Windows in the background.)

The CMOS setup, hard disk partition table, and boot sector are all critical to your computer's operation. Norton Rescue can back up these system boot items to files. Chapter 4, "Getting Started with Norton AntiVirus," covers the details of making a personalized rescue diskette, ready for any emergency.

The Outside

Now that the inside of your computer is cleaned up, it's time to lock the gate and keep it clean. The second half of Strategies for Safe Computing deals with minimizing the outside threats.

Environment

Use a good surge protector to clean up the AC power. The best device for clean AC is a full power-line regulator. Network fileservers need uninterruptable power supplies—but be cautious—during normal operation, many UPSes output dirtier power than they receive from the power receptacle. The UPS's only benefit is to provide some kind of power during a total power blackout. If you require a UPS, be sure to specify a unit that also includes a line regulator to clean up the power.

Dirty power causes slow degradation of electronic components, but a lightning strike or power surge will do immediate damage. Two years ago, lightning struck Paul's office. He had a good line stabilizer on the AC power and it wasn't damaged. However, the modem, system board, parallel port, and HP LaserJet printer were all fried, along with the phone. The moral is... use a surge protector that includes phone line protection.

Support

Build a solid relationship with your support group, whether it is a computer store, corporate information center, micro manager, or user group. One of the great lessons from America's manufacturing sector's current quest for quality is "There is better quality and value when dealing with a single (or few) vendor(s) as opposed to price shopping and bargain hunting."

If the support person knows you and is familiar with your computer, you are more likely to receive better support than if you just bought a drive from a competitor or recently complained to the Director of MIS about your PC.

Users

Avoid letting just anyone use your PC, including the salesman with demo diskettes.

Be sure to scan for viruses whenever your computer service center returns your computer. The diagnostic diskette that booted your computer in the service center has likely been in every misbehaving computer in town.

Passwords

Never share your password (network, accounting software, BBS, CompuServe, or mainframe) with anyone. If a friend needs access to a system, do yourself a favor and recommend your friend to the system's administrator. There is no reason to ever compromise your password.

Never use names or words as passwords. Worms have been known to include a couple thousand popular words. On any given system, someone is bound to use one of these 2,000 words as a password, and by trying the dictionary word as the password, the worm burrows into the system. My suggestion is to use a nonsense word or a non-standard acronym.

Bulletin Boards

Avoid BBSes that distribute pirated (or cracked) software. Do partici-pate with your local PC-User Groups and their BBS. The information and tips you learn will be well worth it. As a rule BBSes don't spread on viruses, they spread virus awareness.

Following is a list of the benefits of a "reputable" BBS:

- Reputable BBSes validate their users and require new users to complete a "New-User Questionnaire." Some BBS SysOps call every user before granting rights to the board. The better BBSes use BBS software that will call you after you call to log in. This call-back feature lets the SysOp further verify the BBS users.

- Reputable BBSes also check software for computer viruses and other rogue software before making it available for downloading. One good way to test this is to upload a file and see how long it takes before the file is available for downloading. It usually takes even the best SysOp a day or two to test all new uploads. Your uploaded file should not appear automatically in the "new up-load" file section.

- Reputable BBSes will often advertise on other local BBSes or in national magazines. Some magazines publish a list annually of reputable BBSes.

- A good way to find reputable BBSes is through the recommenda-tion of other users, User Groups, school affiliations, or affilia-tions with a larger net, such as FIDONet.

Viruses—Keep Out!

There is no sure way to keep your computer from being exposed to rogue software. The place to stop the virus and ANSI bomb is at your disk and diskette drives. The answer is not abstaining from the use of any new software in fear of viruses, but practicing safe computing and using Norton AntiVirus. Also, be sure to keep up with the virus signature updates. An antivirus program that doesn't protect against virus XYZ is useless if that is the virus you are encountering.

Be sure to scan software you have uncompressed. Also, be cautious of self-extracting software (.EXE files that uncompress their contents automatically). They can easily contain an ANSI bomb or a Trojan Horse.

Carefully check any suspicious software. If it claims to be a great new program, but its size is ridiculously small, it's probably a Trojan Horse. Look at the program in Hex or ASCII (using Norton Desktop Viewer or another file-viewing utility) for any messages or ANSI keyboard remapping codes (esc[xx;xxp).

One magazine recently printed an article stating that you should never run any shareware programs unless you saw it run first on someone else's PC to ensure the program was virus- and Trojan Horse-free. The fact is that your friend's computer may or may not show any signs of rogue software. If the shareware software is from a reputable source, shows no viruses when scanned by Virus Clinic, and looks like a program you would enjoy or find productive, go ahead and try it.

If you should detect a computer virus or other rogue software, immediately quarantine the infected PC (take it off the LAN and separate its diskettes). Notify your computer support group. More details about dealing with viruses are in Chapter 6, "Using Virus Clinic."

Summary

Safe computing is understanding the threats and using common sense. Following is a recap of the guidelines for safe computing:

The Inside—where the circuit boards are mounted

- Know your computer.
- Keep your system clean and off the floor.
- Make sure your power supply provides sufficient clean DC power.
- Keep your IRQs / interrupts configured properly.
- Plenty of memory helps the computer run smoother.
- Stay current with an industry standard DOS.
- Delete DOS's FORMAT.COM and FDISK.EXE.
- Rename Norton's Safe Format (SFORMAT.EXE) to NFORMAT.EXE.
- Don't use ANSI.SYS.
- Never boot from a diskette.
- Write-Protect your working copies of DOS.
- Use a good disk-management program, such as Norton Desktop for Windows.
- Keep your directories orderly and logical.
- Fine-tune your disk cache for optimum performance.
- Run Norton Disk Doctor regularly and always use Norton AntiVirus Virus Intercept.
- Keep current with virus signature updates.
- Scan all new software for viruses using Virus Clinic.
- Back up regularly.
- Use Rescue to back up critical system information.

The Outside—where you put the monitor and keyboard

- Use a good surge protector or line stabilizer that includes phone line protection.
- Build a strong working relationship with your computer support group.

- Avoid letting just anyone use your PC.

- Always scan for viruses on any computer returned from the computer service center.

- Don't share your password or use words or names for passwords.

- Check all new software for viruses.

- Avoid unreputable BBSes and do participate with your local PC User Group and their BBS.

Using Norton AntiVirus

Fighting viruses can be a nasty business.

Until the antivirus market matured, the programs used to fight viruses were difficult to use or understand. Information on viruses and their effects was rare and often was more rumor than fact. If you suspected your computer had a virus, you called the best local computer guru you could find and then hoped for the best.

Times have changed. Most computer users have heard of viruses and are aware of their potential danger. As the number of virus attacks increased, more software developers joined the battle against rogue software. This competitive software market benefits the entire computing community as the antivirus developers continually strive to make products safer, comprehensive, and easier to use.

Today, Norton AntiVirus sports an easy-to-use interface with pull-down menus and dialog boxes for DOS users and Windows users. This utility is one of the most complete defenses against attacks by known or unknown viruses.

A Part of this Wholesome Breakfast...

Your personal computer is the product of a complex interaction between hardware made by numerous vendors, its operating system (MS-DOS), software drivers, and any application program. A breakdown or fault in any one of these functions may cause some other component to show symptoms of failure. Often a poorly written software driver, or an ill-configured PC, will cause the computer user to question the equipment's performance. Due to the complex nature of the beast, a holistic approach (one that examines the interrelationships of the whole system) to troubleshooting problems works best.

Computer viruses do cause real problems, and Norton AntiVirus will help you identify and resolve these problems. However, Norton AntiVirus should not be used in a vacuum. Instead, it should be the virus-fighting tool in your toolbox of PC utilities.

Whenever a PC acts strangely, several utilities should be used to isolate all the contributing factors. In addition to Norton AntiVirus, the tools should include Norton Utilities, a general hardware diagnostic program (such as Diagsoft's QA Plus), and specific hardware diagnostics for network interface cards or graphic video cards.

Section II Introduction

Chapter 4, "Getting Started with Norton AntiVirus," is an introduction to Norton AntiVirus and its features. Here we'll step through both the Easy and Advanced Installation options. Installing Norton AntiVirus is half of the preparation, so you'll also create a personalized Rescue diskette.

Virus Intercept is the memory resident portion of Norton AntiVirus. It comes in four different versions, so Chapter 5 will help choose the one that best suits your needs. Also covered are Virus Intercept's virus alerts, what they mean, and how to proceed.

The doctor is in.

Virus Clinic scans and removes viruses from your computer's boot sector or infected program files. Chapter 6, "Using Virus Clinic," presents detailed instructions and explanations on how to make this stressful task easier.

Getting Started with Norton AntiVirus

Norton AntiVirus is a complete system for detecting and fighting viruses. The many programs work in concert to provide comprehensive protection, recovery capabilities, and ease of use.

Virus Intercept guards against viruses, halting the computer and alerting you at the first sign of a software terrorist in your system. Virus Clinic's mission is to "seek and destroy" viruses as it scans and removes them from infected files and disk system areas. Both tasks, guarding against viruses and seeking and destroying viruses, are performed while running MS-DOS or MS-Windows.

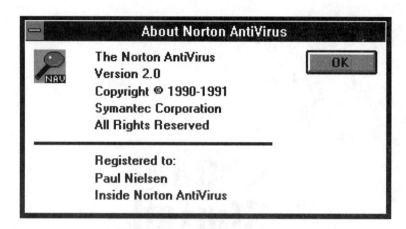

Figure 4-1 Norton AntiVirus 2.0 identification

History of Norton AntiVirus

Norton AntiVirus was first released in December 1990. By August 1991, Version 1.5 added support for virus alerts under Windows. The Peter Norton Group of Symantec considered offering a 1.6 version that would include a Windows version of NAV.EXE, the Virus Clinic scanner, but they opted for a major revision in Norton AntiVirus 2.0. Version 2.0, released in January of 1992, includes many significant improvements. Norton AntiVirus is a mature antivirus tool that provides many features.

In April of 1992, Norton AntiVirus was added to Norton Desktop for Windows and Norton Desktop for DOS.

Norton AntiVirus Features—Comprehensive Virus Identification

At the time this book was going to press, Norton AntiVirus protected against 1,006 strains of 341 known viruses. These include boot-sector infectors, program infectors, and the nastiest of stealth viruses. The "NAV Virus Detection Lab," staffed by Symantec/Peter Norton Group computer engineers who specialize in identifying viruses, constantly provides Norton AntiVirus users with virus definitions as new virus strains are identified. New virus definitions are posted on the Symantec Bulletin Board and the CompuServe Symantec/Norton Utilities Forum.

Transparent Protection

Norton AntiVirus is as unobtrusive as possible. Traditionally, complete virus protection meant constant alerts and warnings. Norton AntiVirus's Virus Intercept inoculates files automatically and does not sound an alert unless there is real cause for alarm. Norton's proprietary methods of file and virus signatures work to eliminate false alarms.

Recursive Testing

Several viruses do not check to see if they have already infected a file before reinfecting it. If a virus has infected your computer for a few weeks, it is possible that every executable program is infected several times over. It is also possible for a program to become infected with more than one virus.

Norton AntiVirus 2.0 handles this problem by performing recursive virus scans. Once a virus is detected in a file, the virus will be reported. During the virus repair step, Norton AntiVirus will continue to scan and repair the infected file until it is satisfied that every virus has been found.

Passive Boot Sector Protection

Norton AntiVirus will optionally alert you any time a program attempts to write to the boot sector of a disk. While it may annoy you to grant permission for the DOS Format command to begin formatting, Norton AntiVirus's watch over the boot sectors can prevent not only a virus but also a Trojan Horse or logic bomb from writing to the partition table or boot sector and corrupting a disk.

Audit Trail and Rescue Capabilities

Virus Intercept records viral activity as text in an audit trail. This history can prove invaluable while hunting down a virus in a large diverse multi-LAN installation.

While the chance that a new virus strain or Trojan Horse program would attack your computer is incredibly slim, the Norton Rescue program makes it easier to recover the system areas of your disk from a disaster. In three files, Norton Rescue stores a copy of your CMOS set-up information, hard-disk partition data, and boot sectors.

Windows and Local Area Networks

Norton AntiVirus for Windows makes fighting viruses easier while running Windows. NAVW.EXE is a Windows version of the Norton AntiVirus Virus Clinic, and NPOPUP.EXE reports viruses found by Virus Intercept.

Norton AntiVirus also works cooperatively with most popular networks, such as Novell Netware 286 or 386, 3COM 3+Open, OS/2 LAN Manager, Banyan Vines, and AT&T Starlan networks. Its flexible configuration, options, and password protection allow LAN administrators to control the virus security efforts on the LAN.

Hardware Requirements

Every MS-DOS based computer is capable of running Norton AntiVirus. Specifically, Norton AntiVirus requires the computer to meet the following specifications:

- 384Kb RAM

- DOS 3.1 or greater

- 538Kb Minimal Installation for DOS (without Windows support)

- 800Kb Normal Installation

- 990Kb Normal Installation with the files expanded

Installation

Preparing to fight viruses with Norton AntiVirus is a twofold process. First, Norton AntiVirus needs to be installed and your system certified as *virus-free*. You'll find the install program is straightforward, explains every step, makes no unannounced alterations to your system, and is a breeze to go through. Once Norton AntiVirus is up and running, the next step is to create a personalized *Rescue Diskette*, part of a software toolbox of the utilities needed to troubleshoot any unforeseen problem.

Norton AntiVirus's automatic installation will walk you through the process with easily understandable dialog boxes that explain every step.

If you currently use Norton AntiVirus and are upgrading to version 2.0, stop and disable Virus Intercept. To do this step, reboot your computer and press and hold down both Shift keys as soon as the computer sounds the start-up beep. To install Norton AntiVirus, follow these steps:

1. Insert the Norton AntiVirus diskette #1 in the diskette drive, switch to the diskette drive (assuming you are using A:), and then run the install program.

   ```
   C>A:<enter>

   A>INSTALL<enter>
   ```

2. Choose the type of video display: monochrome or color.

3. Scan for viruses.

   We strongly recommend that you begin by scanning for viruses. Many viruses give no indication of their presence until the damage is done. The safe course of action is to ensure you begin with a clean, non-infected machine.

4. Remove old inoculation files. Prior to Norton AntiVirus version 2.0, each executable file had an inoculation file. Version 2.0 uses only one inoculation file. It's only necessary to remove the inoculation files if you previously used Norton AntiVirus version 1.0 or 1.5.

NOTE: The installation program for Norton AntiVirus includes an option for removing the inoculation files. Norton Desktop's installation, however, does not automate this step. If you are upgrading from Norton AntiVirus 1.0 or 1.5 to Norton Desktop's AntiVirus 2.0, use Norton AntiVirus 1.0 or 1.5's UNINOC.EXE program to remove the inoculation files.

5. Confirm or change the directory to which you want to install Norton AntiVirus.

   For the sake of keeping the DOS path short, we recommend keeping it in \NAV.

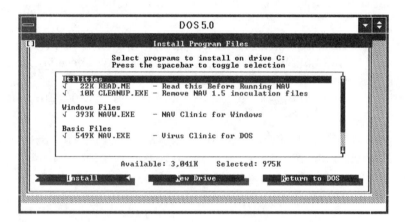

Figure 4-2 Installation options

6. Select the portions of Norton AntiVirus you want to install.

   Only two items are truly optional: CLEANUP.EXE and NAVW.EXE. If you didn't run version 1.0 or 1.5 of Norton AntiVirus, you do not need CLEANUP.EXE. The NAVW.EXE file provides support for Windows. If you don't run Windows, you can skip installing NAVW.EXE. If you choose to run Windows later, you can add the files then.

7. Save the Rescue data. The Rescue program, also included in Norton Utilities, is critical to the overall Norton plan for safe computing. You can save this data now, or save it in a few minutes when we build your personalized Rescue Diskette.

Easy Installation

The installation program now branches into two paths: the Easy Installation and the Advanced Installation. Regardless of which you choose, the same files are copied to your hard disk. The difference is the Easy Installation sets options to the most common (or popular) defaults while the Advanced Installation permits you to fully customize Norton AntiVirus. The Easy Installation sets the following options:

- Installs Virus Intercept as a memory-resident device driver to watch for viruses. It chooses the 4K version of Virus Intercept that is recommended for most users. This version of Virus Intercept finds viruses during all program executions and scans diskettes for boot-sector viruses. The 4K version does not scan for viruses during file copies and does not write-protect the system areas of your disk.

- Adds a command to your AUTOEXEC.BAT to scan memory and your root directory for viruses. This scan is highly recommended and will help catch any boot-sector viruses.

- \NAV is added to your DOS path, and a NAV environment variable is set (Set Nav = \NAV) to help Virus Clinic find NAV_.SYS. Also, the default colors and mouse options are selected automatically.

Advanced Installation

The Advanced Installation presents a menu of items that can be customized (see figure 4-3). All of these options can be reconfigured later by running the NAVSETUP program, modifying CONFIG.SYS, or choosing the Options menu in Virus Clinic (NAV.EXE). Following are the Advanced Installation options:

- Video options enable you to select a color set, the number of lines on the screen, the amount of graphics used, the screen background, and the type of command buttons. The mouse options enable you to set the double-clicking sensitivity of the mouse, movement speed, and reset speed.

- The Advanced Installation lets you select the Virus Intercept version and initial scan easily without having to edit CONFIG.SYS or AUTOEXEC.BAT. Optionally, the installation program will show you the changes the installation made to CONFIG.SYS and AUTOEXEC.BAT and let you make additional edits.

- The Norton AntiVirus files are installed on your disk as compressed files. They expand themselves as you run them; this can cause a second or two delay. The choice is yours: You can expand the files during installation and speed up program loading, or save about 150Kb of your disk. Over the course of a year, you will only spend a couple of minutes waiting. It depends on your priorities, your computer disk speed, and how long you've had your hard disk. (If you decide to expand the files later, NAVSETUP.EXE will accommodate you. Once the files are expanded, however, they can not be recompressed.)

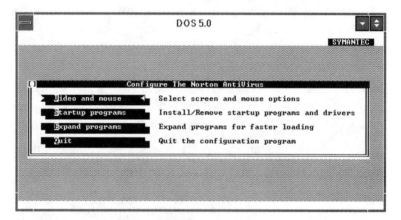

Figure 4-3 Advanced Installation options

Personal Preferences

While this book was being written, we used two computers side-by-side; one for running Word for Windows and the other for testing controlled viral infections. Some days, the test system would be infected and rebuilt 10 to 15 times. Several diagnostic diskettes were transferred between the word processing system and the test system. All this went on during the trigger days of the Michelangelo, Jerusalem, and Maltese Amoeba viruses. To ensure that my main PC didn't become infected accidentally, we continuously ran the Comprehensive Scan version of Virus Intercept (NAV_.SYS /W) and scanned

COMMAND.COM during AUTOEXEC.BAT. We also carefully scanned all the test diskettes from time to time.

Building the Rescue Diskette

One of the key principles of fighting viruses is that it is easier to re-move a virus infection when the virus is not running in memory. If you should encounter a virus, Norton AntiVirus will recommend that you turn off the power to the PC, reboot with a known clean (virus-free) copy of DOS, and then run Virus Clinic. Chances are that you'll see a hardware problem or a corrupt FAT (File Allocation Table) before you see a virus. For either case, your Rescue Diskettes should represent a collection of your favorite utilities, ready for any problem (see table). Figure 4-4 displays a sample Rescue Diskstte.

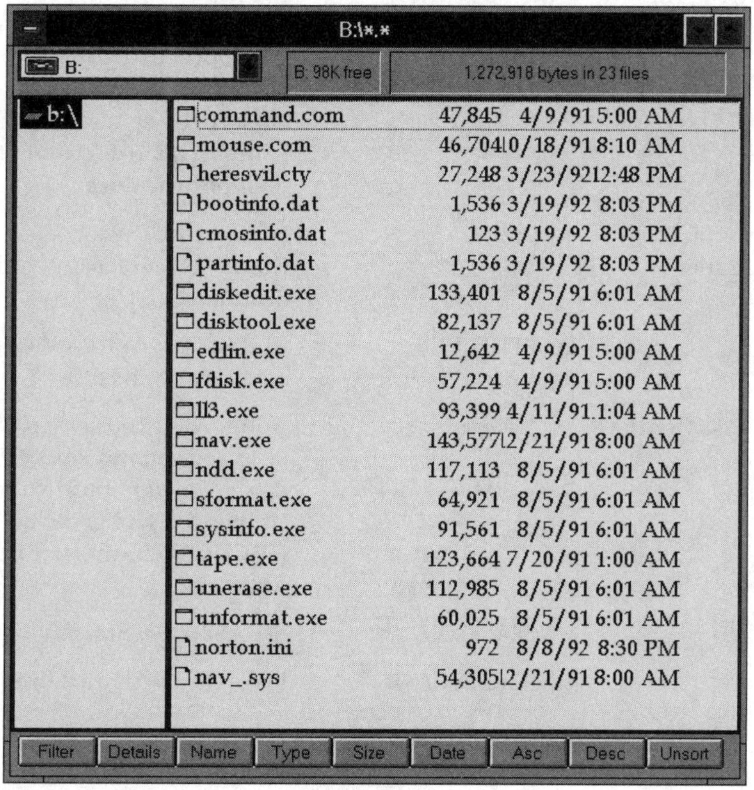

B:*.*		
B:	B: 98K free	1,272,918 bytes in 23 files

b:\			
	command.com	47,845	4/9/91 5:00 AM
	mouse.com	46,704	10/18/91 8:10 AM
	heresvil.cty	27,248	3/23/92 12:48 PM
	bootinfo.dat	1,536	3/19/92 8:03 PM
	cmosinfo.dat	123	3/19/92 8:03 PM
	partinfo.dat	1,536	3/19/92 8:03 PM
	diskedit.exe	133,401	8/5/91 6:01 AM
	disktool.exe	82,137	8/5/91 6:01 AM
	edlin.exe	12,642	4/9/91 5:00 AM
	fdisk.exe	57,224	4/9/91 5:00 AM
	il3.exe	93,399	4/11/91.1:04 AM
	nav.exe	143,577	12/21/91 8:00 AM
	ndd.exe	117,113	8/5/91 6:01 AM
	sformat.exe	64,921	8/5/91 6:01 AM
	sysinfo.exe	91,561	8/5/91 6:01 AM
	tape.exe	123,664	7/20/91 1:00 AM
	unerase.exe	112,985	8/5/91 6:01 AM
	unformat.exe	60,025	8/5/91 6:01 AM
	norton.ini	972	8/8/92 8:30 PM
	nav_.sys	54,305	12/21/91 8:00 AM

| Filter | Details | Name | Type | Size | Date | Asc | Desc | Unsort |

Figure 4-4 Norton Desktop view of Rescue Diskette

Source	Program/Filename	Purpose/Comment
DOS 5.0	MSDOS.SYS, IO.SYS and COMMAND.COM	Format the diskette with the /S switch to copy the system files and COMMAND.COM.
	FDISK.EXE	Creates disk partitions and freshens the partition table.
	EDLIN.EXE	Basic Line Editor—DOS 5's Edit is much better; however, it requires QBASIC.EXE (255Kb).
NAV	NAV.EXE	Virus Clinic—Finds and removes viruses.
	NAV_.SYS	Virus Intercept—Contains virus definitions.
Rescue Files	PARTINFO.DAT, BOOTINFO.DAT, and CMOSINFO.DAT	Use DISKTOOL.EXE, RESCUE.EXE, or Virus Clinic (NAV.EXE) to create the Rescue Files. Each PC's Rescue Files will be unique, so be sure to use separate directories for multiple machines.
Norton Utilities	NDD.EXE	Norton Disk Doctor— Diagnoses and repairs hard disk faults.
	DISKEDIT.EXE	Norton Disk Editor—Views anything on the disk.
DISKTOOL.EXE		Norton Disk Tools—Repairs disks and restores Rescue data files. If you don't use Norton Utilities, be sure to include RESCUE.EXE from Norton AntiVirus.
	UNERASE.EXE	Recovers deleted files.
	UNFORMAT.EXE	Recovers a formatted disk.

Source	Program/Filename	Purpose/Comment
	SYSINFO.EXE	Norton SI—Classic program that determines system specifications and status.
	SFORMAT	Norton Safe Format.
DiagSoft, Inc.	QAPlus	Hardware tester.
	Tape Backup/Restore software	To restore data, in case of the worst. In my case—TAPE.EXE.
Computer Manufacturer	SETUP.EXE	Some PCs require a diskette from the manufacturer to set the CMOS system configuration.

If you are familiar with the programs listed, chances are that you have already created your personal PC utility toolkit similar to this one. However, even if you are not adept at the inner details of Norton Disk Doctor II, it is still a good idea to make a Rescue Diskette (see the following table). Many technical programs are becoming more intelligent and are easy to use. Even if you call in a PC expert during a crisis, having the critical files ready will increase the chance of a successful repair.

Command	Explanation
NAV_.SYS	Reboot and press and hold both Shift keys at the startup beep. This disables Virus Intercept so that NAV_.SYS can be copied.
NAV C:	Scan the hard disk to ensure the system is virus-free before the Rescue Diskette is created.
FORMAT A: /S	Prepare the disk and make it bootable.

Command	Explanation
NAV C:	Cancel the scan, select the Create Rescue Disk option from the Tools menu, confirm creating the Rescue Diskette, and select the A: drive. Make a backup copy of your boot sector, partition table, and CMOS setup configuration.
COPY C:\DOS\MEM.EXE A:	Copy the necessary DOS programs. (You will need to substitute your own correct paths here.)
COPY C:\DOS\FORMAT.EXE A:	
COPY C:\DOS\FDISK.EXE A:	
COPY C:\DOS\EDLIN.EXE A:	
COPY C:\NORTON\SFORMAT.EXE A:	These are the repair tools of Norton Utilities. (Again, you'll need to substitute your own paths to the Norton files if they are in a different location than we show here.)
COPY C:\NORTON\NDD.EXE A:	
COPY C:\NORTON\DISKEDIT.EXE	
COPY C:\NORTON\DISKTOOL.EXE A:	
COPY C:\NORTON\SYSINFO.EXE A:	
COPY C:\NORTON\UNERASE.EXE A:	
COPY C:\NORTON\UNFORMAT.EXE A:	
COPY C:\<Other> A:	Make a copy of your favorite Disk Manager (Norton Commander or XTreeGold), Hardware Diagnostic Program, Memory Manager/ Viewer, or Backup (Tape) Restore Program.

Once the Rescue Diskette is complete, write-protect it with a tape tab or engage the sliding tab and store it in a safe place.

Often the computer manufacturer's documentation is only consulted during a crisis or problem. Because that is where you are likely to look, the Rescue Diskette would easily be found in a box near those computer books.

Summary

Norton AntiVirus is a mature virus-fighting utility, providing a balance of thorough transparent protection, compatibility with DOS, Windows and LANs, and ease of operation. As with any utility, different programs perform different tasks. To combat computer terrorists effectively, Virus Intercept warns of virus sightings and Virus Clinic seeks and destroys viruses. These programs, used in partnership, can provide a sound defense against computer viruses.

We wear seat belts to limit the danger of an auto accident, and we take precautions when warned of storms or tornadoes. Yet neither of these dangers are actually plotted against us. It takes planning to defend against such a threat. The best planning includes careful system configuration, including Virus Intercept and Virus Clinic, and a good toolbox of utilities, including the Rescue Diskette.

Using Virus Intercept

What is Virus Intercept?

Norton AntiVirus uses a multi-pronged defense against viruses. *Virus Intercept* is the portion of Norton AntiVirus that resides in memory, watching files as they are read from the disk and anticipating a virus attack. Virus Intercept does not remove viruses or repair files. If a virus is found by Virus Intercept, the utility Virus Clinic (NAV.EXE) must be used to repair or delete the infected program.

The following Virus Intercept identification notice, displayed as Virus Intercept, is loaded by CONFIG.SYS and identifies the operating version of Virus Intercept being loaded.

```
The Norton AntiVirus

Version 2.0

Comprehensive Scan

Copyright 1989-1991 by

Symantec Corporation

All Rights Reserved
```

Virus Intercept scans files as DOS reads them from the disk during file copies and application launches. If a virus is found, Virus Intercept halts all computer activity, sounds a siren through the PC speaker, and displays a rather large red alert box announcing the virus and offers you a chance to avoid becoming a virus statistic. (It's easy to become accustomed to pressing Enter automatically to continue after any delay. The Virus Intercept siren and red alert box are designed to get your attention so that you don't just press Enter. Because Virus Intercept is programmed to operate as unobtrusively as possible, you should not see many false alarms.)

Virus Intercept also watches for boot-sector viruses by intercepting the warm-boot keystroke combination (Ctrl+Alt+Del), and then scanning the A: floppy drive for a boot-sector virus. Boot-sector viruses, like Stoned and Michelangelo, can only infect a PC if the PC boots from an infected diskette in a floppy drive. In this way, Virus Intercept protects against the boot-sector viruses that lurk on the diskette that you may have left in the floppy drive.

Slim as it may be, there is always a chance that you may come across a new virus strain before the NAV Virus Detection Lab has identified it and released a virus definition. Norton AntiVirus protects against unknown viruses two ways. First, Virus Intercept monitors executable files and reports any changes. Second, Virus Intercept can write-protect the hard disk's partition table and also the boot sector of the hard disk and diskette.

This write-protection defends against more than just a boot-sector virus; other rogue software (Trojan Horses, ANSI bombs, and logic bombs) can also tamper with the partition table and boot sector.

As a device driver, Virus Intercept takes up valuable RAM. Therefore, Norton AntiVirus includes three different versions of Virus Intercept (NAV_.SYS, NAV&.SYS /b, and NAV&.SYS) with varying levels of protection, disk performance and memory consumption. Lastly, Virus Intercept can leave an audit trail of its activity in a specified file.

Loading Virus Intercept

Virus Intercept should be the first device driver loaded immediately upon booting the computer. This lets Virus Intercept watch for viruses while the other drivers, programs, and batch files are loading.

Virus Intercept may be loaded in one of several different configurations. Only one copy of Virus Intercept may be active. Any subsequent attempts to load Virus Intercept will be ignored.

> **NOTE:** It is possible to prohibit Virus Intercept from loading. This can be handy when you want to copy NAV_.SYS to a Rescue Diskette or to track system conflicts (Virus Intercept stops any attempts to read NAV_.SYS). When the PC is first powered on the bootstrap program in the BIOS, it will normally give one beep. Immediately, hold down both shift keys until the following message appears.

```
Norton AntiVirus not loaded

Copyright 1989-1991 by

Symantec Corporation

All Rights Reserved
```

You can disable Virus Clinic by pressing and holding down both Shift keys during the boot sequence.

Execute Only Scan — NAV&.SYS

The smallest version of Virus Intercept, NAV&.SYS uses only 1K of RAM and detects a virus as the infected application is executed. It provides no protection against boot-sector viruses nor does it detect viruses during file-copy operations. This version of Virus Intercept is well suited to a computer system with several memory resident programs already tight on RAM.

If you seldom swap diskettes and are not concerned about boot-sector protection, the 1K Virus Intercept does a good job of stopping a program-infector virus from becoming live in memory.

NOTE: If you run Windows, the 1K version of Virus Intercept does not establish communications with NAVPOPUP.EXE (the Windows portion of Virus Intercept) and therefore does not present a Windows dialog box for virus alerts. If you get a virus alert while in Windows, Virus Intercept will present the normal red alert box and sound as a full-screen DOS application.

A diskless LAN workstation is an ideal candidate for this version of Virus Clinic. Without a diskette drive, the workstation cannot introduce a program-infecting virus to the LAN, nor can it attempt to boot from a boot-sector virus-infected diskette.

Execute and Boot Scan—NAV&.SYS /b and Comprehensive Scan—NAV_.SYS

The NAV&.SYS /b version, at 6K, also saves memory and adds the capability to scan for boot-sector viruses before a warm boot (Ctrl+Alt+Del). For many users (especially Windows fans), this version provides the best balance of protection and performance. This is the default version loaded by the Easy Installation.

NAV_.SYS is the most complete version of Virus Clinic. It adds detection of viruses during file-copy operations, and the option of write-protecting the system areas of the disk. This version also contains the virus definitions, so that it does not need to load them during the boot process. While this version occupies more memory than the other versions, it provides the highest level of virus protection. If you tend to test-drive much software, NAV_.SYS provides the level of virus protection you need.

The actual amount of memory that NAV_.SYS requires depends on the number of virus definitions loaded.

/W (Write Protect option)	Instructs NAV_.SYS to alert you whenever an attempt is made to write to the first two sectors of the hard disk (partition table and boot sector), or the first sector of a floppy diskette (boot sector). Only NAV_.SYS can use this option.

/A (Alternate Boot option)   Switches the boot-sector virus
                              scan from the A: drive to the B:
                              drive. This switch may be used
                              with the NAV_.SYS device
                              driver or the NAV&.SYS /b
                              version of Virus Intercept.

Performance Considerations

Virus Intercept directly affects computer speed performance by scanning the files as they are read from the disk. Depending on the configuration, Virus Intercept can affect the efficient performance of other programs indirectly by lowering the amount of available memory.

Which Virus Intercept Is Right for You?

The selection of which version of Virus Intercept to load depends on the following factors:

- Are you at risk for a virus attack?

- If Virus Intercept is to be loaded without the benefit of a memory manager, how much conventional memory is required by your application software?

- With a memory manager, how much high memory is available after other device drivers are loaded high?

- How often do you make backups? If your hard disk was zapped, what would it cost you in time or money?

If you don't often experiment with new software, NAV&.SYS /b provides adequate protection without sacrificing performance or memory. On the other hand, if you tend to try new software regularly, NAV_.SYS's Write Protect option could save your hard disk from not only a virus attack but also from the attack of a Trojan Horse program.

Examples of the CONFIG.SYS File

Virus Intercept is loaded from CONFIG.SYS. If you are not familiar
with CONFIG.SYS, it is the file in the root directory of the boot drive
that sets DOS's internal configuration. CONFIG.SYS commands are
executed when the PC is first started, before COMMAND.COM is
loaded and before AUTOEXEC.BAT commands are executed. Following are some examples of statements you might use in CONFIG.SYS
with Virus Intercept:

Statement	Explanation
DEVICE = C:\NAV\NAV_.SYS /W	Loads the comprehensive version of Virus Intercept with the Write Protect option.
DEVICEHIGH = C:\NAV\NAV_.SYS	Uses the DOS 5.0 memory management features to load Virus Intercept into high memory.
DEVICE = C:\NAV\NAV&.SYS /B /A	Loads the 6K version of Virus Intercept which checks for boot viruses on the B: drive.
DEVICE = C:\QEMM\LOADHI	Uses Quarterdeck's QEMM /R:2 C:\NAV\NAV_.SYS Memory Manager's LoadHigh driver to load NAV_.SYS into high memory.

NOTE: QEMM386.SYS must be loaded before Virus Intercept can be
loaded into high memory with LOADHI.SYS. The /R parameter
instructs QEMM to load the device driver in the second high-
memory region. Use Quarterdeck's Optimize program to determine the best high-memory region for your system.

Troubleshooting Loading Problems

Virus Intercept likes to "take over" several aspects of the PC so that a virus cannot sneak past detection. It is possible that Virus Intercept may conflict with another driver your computer loads after Virus Intercept.

When Paul first loaded Norton AntiVirus, he found that his machine would completely hang right after displaying the Virus Intercept loaded message. It turned out that a couple lines later in CONFIG.SYS, RAMBIOS.SYS, a driver for his ATI Graphics Ultra videoboard was causing the conflict. The ATI video-driver software was relocating video ROM to faster RAM and definitely conflicted with NAV_.SYS.

To resolve the preceding conflict, follow these steps:

1. Remove every statement, except the statement that loads Virus Intercept from CONFIG.SYS, by placing a REM (or remark) command before the statements. If you press and hold down both Shift keys right after the beep as the computer starts, Virus Intercept will not load. This enables you to bypass the conflict and get to DOS to run your editor.

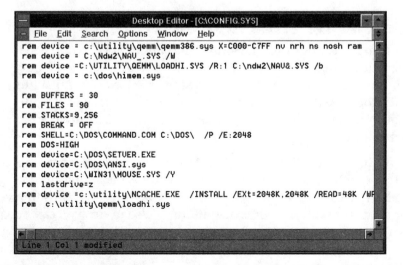

Figure 5-1 A clean CONFIG.SYS, ready for device driver conflict testing

2. Rename AUTOEXEC.BAT to AUTOEXEC.NAV.

3. Reboot your system.

   If NAV_.SYS still won't load and your system employs any shadow RAM techniques (makes a copy or shadow of the ROM-BIOS or video-BIOS in faster system RAM), try turning off the system Shadow RAM on the mother board or CMOS setup.

4. One at a time, add the device drivers back into CONFIG.SYS by removing the REM command until you find the program that is causing the conflict.

5. Now that you have identified the culprit, you need to decide if it is a critical file. Maybe you can do without it (as Paul did with the conflicting ATI video driver). Another option may be to load the conflicting software in the form of a .COM file. For example, many mouse drivers have sister executable files. You could load MOUSE.SYS in CONFIG.SYS or MOUSE.COM in AUTOEXEC.BAT.

6. If the solution isn't obvious, don't hesitate to give the Peter Norton Group Tech Support a call at (310) 453-4600.

7. Once the problem is worked out, rename AUTOEXEC.NAV back to AUTOEXEC.BAT.

Defending Virus Intercept

Norton AntiVirus stores the virus signatures in NAV_.SYS. The virus signatures are used by Virus Clinic and Virus Intercept to identify viruses. If a stealth virus was designed to attack Norton AntiVirus, this would be the file it would attempt to alter. That's why Norton AntiVirus defends NAV_.SYS like a Los Angeles class fast-attack submarine.

Virus Intercept will return an `Invalid Device Request reading device NAV_.SYS` error message if any attempt is made to read or write to NAV_.SYS. This keeps rogue software from infecting Virus Intercept or tampering with the virus definitions. It also means you can't copy NAV_.SYS unless you keep Virus Intercept from loading by pressing and holding down both Shift keys immediately after the beep during the boot process.

Virus Intercept does a good job of watching disk-reads to prevent a virus from entering memory; however, a boot-sector virus would load into memory before DOS's CONFIG.SYS could load Virus Intercept. Virus Intercept would be too late to see a boot-sector virus load into memory from an infected hard disk. Virus Intercept's defense against boot-sector viruses comes many stages earlier, preventing the initial infection.

For example, Virus Intercept will detect Michelangelo on an infected diskette (the boot-sector virus that became a media event prior to March 6th, 1992). But Virus Intercept, without Virus Clinic, would not sound an alert once the hard disk was infected.

To protect against boot-sector viruses, follow these steps:

1. Add NAV C:\ to AUTOEXEC.BAT. This will scan memory as well as any programs in your root directory (including COMMAND.COM) and detect a boot-sector virus already hiding in memory. If you chose the Easy Installation, it placed this command in AUTOEXEC.BAT automatically. Alternately, you could perform a full scan during AUTOEXEC.BAT, but realistically, that would take too long.

2. Scan diskettes before booting from them. NAV_.SYS /W makes this easy by scanning the A: drive automatically before a warm boot.

NAV_.SYS File Attributes

Because Virus Intercept protects NAV_.SYS, it is not necessary to mark this file READ-ONLY. In fact, Norton AntiVirus writes configuration and virus definition information in NAV_.SYS so that you don't need to set NAV_.SYS to READ-ONLY.

Alerts

Virus Intercept will sound an alert and display a red dialog box when it detects a virus or virus-like activity. The sound can be disabled in the Options menu of Virus Clinic.

The options that an Alert provides can be tailored within the configuration dialog boxes. This enables you to specify the following options:

- Whether alerts can be bypassed with the proceed button.

- Enable an alert to sound the alarm.

- Specification of the pop-up alert box and for what amount of time the display should remain on-screen before Norton AntiVirus cancels the action automatically and permits the computer to continue.

- The way in which uninoculated files should be handled: automatic inoculation or inoculation by the user.

- Whether a log of all Virus Intercept alerts is kept.

- Assigning filenames.

- Detection of unknown viruses.

- Which files should be scanned (all files or just the executable files).

- Customized warning messages, such as "Call the MIS Dept. ASAP at phone extension 1234."

Virus Intercept Alert

Figure 5-2 The Norton AntiVirus Scan Results Intercept dialog box

A Virus Intercept alert means that Norton AntiVirus has identified a virus during a disk- or diskette-read operation by matching a virus definition with the virus's tell-tale signature in the infected file. The purpose of the alert is two-fold.

The alert gives you a chance to cancel the file-copy or program-execute operation. This keeps the virus from entering memory and infecting more files. Virus Intercept completely halts all computer activity, preventing further activity of a virus which might already be in memory.

Now that a virus has been identified, the infected file should be deleted or repaired. Virus Clinic, the scan-and-repair portion of Norton AntiVirus, will repair or delete the infection.

NOTE: Once Virus Intercept finds a virus, be sure to scan the entire disk again, not just the infected file. If virus intercept has not been active, the virus may have already spread.

Boot-Sector Alert

A boot-sector virus alert warns that the diskette in the drive is infected. If the alert is sounded (a boot-sector alert will sound the siren even if the sound option is disabled) during a file copy or program execution from a diskette, it is safe to proceed with the disk-read operation. This may be somewhat confusing; however, a boot-sector virus can only infect a PC if you attempt to boot from the infected floppy diskette, regardless of whether the diskette is a bootable DOS diskette. Every time the PC is warm booted (press Ctrl+Alt+Del), Virus Intercept looks to the A: drive to check for the presence of a boot-sector virus. The red alert box should flash momentarily as Virus Intercept becomes active. If no virus is found, the warm boot continues. If a virus is found on the diskette, Virus Intercept will not permit you to continue until the diskette is removed from the drive; otherwise, the boot-sector virus would surely infect the hard disk.

NOTE: The best response to a boot-sector virus alert is to run Virus Clinic and remove the virus from the infected diskette. Alternately, it is safe to copy the data files from the diskette and reformat the diskette using the DOS format or Norton Utilities' Safe Format in the destructive format mode.

Inoculation Change

A program-infector virus must attach itself to a file, thereby changing the infected file's length, or rewrite a part of the file, which changes the file's signature value. A *file-signature* checksum is a complex proprietary method of identifying changes to a file. The file signature looks at file size and contents, specifically the portions of the program file that a virus would need to change when infecting a file. Virus Intercept uses the file signature to monitor the integrity of a file. If the Auto-Inoculate option is on the first time an executable program is launched, Virus Intercept calculates the file signature and records it.

If the file signature of the file is altered, Virus Intercept will warn you with an Inoculation Change Alert box. This alert warns of a change in the program file that may be caused by an unknown (undocumented) virus or file corruption.

The Inoculation Change Alert may not always be indicating a virus. It is possible that the program file in question has been changed legitimately. Perhaps the program's configuration was altered or the file was updated. Virus Intercept will alert you that the file has been changed and give you the option of saving the new file signature as a new inoculation for the file.

If you can find no reason to explain the change in the file's checksum, you can assume that the file has been infected with a virus, or at the very least has been corrupted. Virus Intercept reported an Inoculation Change but did not report a virus attack, so it is possible that you are discovering a new virus strain.

An inoculation alert will also be generated if a program has been moved to a new directory or the directory has been renamed. Turning on the Auto-Inoculate option in Virus Clinic's Global Options will prevent this annoyance.

Use CLEANUP.EXE to remove the individual file signatures used by earlier versions of Norton AntiVirus.

Norton AntiVirus's file-signature method is an advancement over the basic checksum method of detecting a change in a file. A little technical information about basic checksums: a checksum is a count of the number of set bits or binary "1's" in a file (at the lowest level, all files are made of 1's and 0's). The traditional checksum method places this total in one byte, ignoring any overflow. Only the least significant byte (or 8 bit remainder) is retained. For example, if the total number of bits set in a file was 654,32110 (base 10 or decimal) or 9 FBF116 (base 16 or hexadecimal), the checksum or least significant byte would be 116.

A basic checksum is like checking an odometer reading by looking at only the last two digits of the odometer reading on the registration. It might catch an accidental error, but it wouldn't foil an unscrupulous used car dealer from turning back the odometer without changing the last two digits!

This method of checksum validation is a satisfactory proof of accidental data corruption during data transmission. The problem is that a virus isn't accidental. Theoretically, a virus could calculate the basic checksum of a targeted file. Then, if the virus inserted itself into the target file, the virus could easily write one to seven 1's into the file to adjust the checksum total such that the 1 byte remainder remained the same. The file length is unaltered and the checksum remains intact. The result is a well-hidden stealth virus. (The Fish-6 virus goes beyond this simple stealth method. It evades detection by full CRC checksum methods. Nevertheless, Norton AntiVirus detected a change in a program file we infected with the Fish-6 virus while preparing this book. We removed the Fish-6 virus signature previously so that Norton AntiVirus had to detect the virus by only the infected file's file-signature change.)

That's why Norton AntiVirus uses a complex, proprietary, and encrypted file-signature method of testing the integrity of a file.

The next question concerns where the file-signature data should be stored. One popular antivirus technique is to append a file's checksum data to the end of that same file. This leaves the data open to investigation by a virus and alerts the virus that the file has been inoculated. A virus could easily remove the checksum data from the file and infect the file. The antivirus software would see the infected file as a new file, without checksum data. It would happily perform a checksum and believe the file was now protected. This method could actually provide camouflage for a new virus!

Rest assured, the Norton AntiVirus developers are one step ahead. Virus Intercept stores the file-signature data in a hidden file and carefully guards it from any tampering by prohibiting all reads and writes to the file.

Write-Protect Alert

If the NAV_.SYS version of Virus Intercept is loaded with the /W option, the Write-Protect Alert is enabled. Any time a program attempts to write directly to the boot sectors or partition table of any disk or diskette, Virus Intercept displays the Write-Protect Alert. Several DOS operations normally write to the boot sector. In addition to monitoring viral activity, the Write-Protect Alert would also warn you in the event of an accidental disk format.

The following programs will normally write to the boot sector:

- Norton Disk Doctor (NDD.EXE—during repair)
- Norton Disk Editor (DISKEDIT.EXE)
- DOS LABEL
- Any program that changes the Volume Label
- FDISK
- DOS Format or Norton Safe Format—any hard drive or diskette

A technical note about Write-Protect Alerts and multiple logical drives—if the hard disk is partitioned into three or more DOS drives, the second and consecutive drives are logical partitions of the same extended partition in the partition table. Therefore, formatting any of the logical drives will cause a /W alert for the first logical drive in the extended partition. For example, drive C: is the primary partition and drive D: and E: are logical drives of the same extended partition. Formatting drive E: will cause a boot sector Write Protect Alert for the D: drive.

If there is no good reason why an attempt was made to write to a boot sector, then certainly do not permit the offending program to proceed. You may be seeing the attack of a Trojan Horse program, or (because Virus Intercept did not identify a virus when sounding the alert) you may have discovered a new virus strain. As with an unexplained checksum change, refer to Chapter 6, "Using Virus Clinic," for more information.

Compatibility Issues and Solutions

Virus Intercept checks for viruses during disk reads, not during disk writes. This line of defense prevents viruses from loading into memory where they can activate and replicate, and provides the most thorough protection against viruses without sacrificing performance. There are a few cases in which an infected file can get on the hard disk; however, Virus Intercept will alert you as soon as the infected program is executed. This keeps the virus from spreading or damaging your software.

Other issues concerning Virus Intercept involve compatibility with certain programs. Most of these problems arise with time-sensitive programs, such as communication software or programs that directly move the contents of memory.

Compressed Files

If a virus is attached to a program that has been compressed with PKZIP or LHARC or any other file-compression utility program, the virus signature is unlikely to be found in the compressed file. Virus Intercept will not sound an alarm when the compressed file containing the virus is copied to the hard disk.

Furthermore, Virus Intercept will not notice the virus until the file is decompressed, and then copied or executed. Here's why. When PKUNZIP.EXE (for example) decompresses a file, Virus Intercept cannot identity the virus signature as the compressed file is read from the disk. PKUNZIP decompresses the file in memory and writes it back to the disk. Virus Intercept still has not yet had an opportunity to identify the file during a disk read. Of course, Virus Intercept will locate the virus when the program is executed or copied, and will protect you from a virus attack.

This scenario would be a rare case. You would have to copy the zipped file to a diskette or unzip the file to a diskette, and then pass the diskette to another user. Virus protection, however, will not have had an opportunity (in this scenario) to detect the virus from the unzipped file on the diskette.

The illustrated batch file below, UNZIP.BAT, helps in the case of the "compressed virus" scenario. It simply runs Norton AntiVirus's Virus Clinic after uncompressing files. The batch file assumes the compression-uncompression utility is PKZIP and that PKUNZIP.EXE is in the \UTILITY directory. (You'll need to make changes to reflect your own setup.) The Batch file should be in a directory that is included in the DOS Path.

```
UNZIP.BAT
@ECHO OFF
c:\utility\PKUNZIP %1
C:\NAV\NAV *.*
```

A *self-extracting zip file* is a collection of compressed files in the form of an executable file. The .ZIP compressed file has been appended or joined with a small program that unzips or uncompresses the zip file automatically. They present the same problems as zip files. Additionally, the executable portion could possibly be infected by a virus, which Virus Intercept would find.

What appears to be a self-extracting file may be a Trojan Horse or hide an ANSI bomb. If you suspect the self-extracting file for any reason, use your regular compression utility (PKUNZip, LHA, PKXArc) to uncompress the file. A self-extracting file does not have to be self-extracted.

Downloaded Files

Files that are downloaded from a BBS or CompuServe are not seen by Virus Intercept until they are executed later. Just as with compressed files, it is prudent to scan them with Virus Clinic before distributing them to other PCs. Any other tool that loads files directly to the disk, such as LapLink, Brooklyn Bridge, Commander Link, or CloseUp, can also bypass Virus Intercept.

High-Speed Backup and Restore

Some tape backup programs may conflict with Virus Intercept. If you have any problems, the easiest solution may be to back up when Virus Intercept isn't loaded. Press and hold down both Shift keys after the bootstrap beep to keep Virus Intercept from loading. If you restore without Virus Intercept loaded, be sure to scan your disk with Virus Clinic before you run any programs.

If your tape backup program runs fine with Virus Intercept loaded, keep these two items in mind:

- When backing up to tape, don't mark NAV_.SYS for backup. Remember, NAV_.SYS can't be read to or written to while Virus Intercept is active. Virus Intercept prevents the file read, and the backup program may respond as if the disk is no longer available.

- If "Detect Uninoculated Files" is on and "Auto-Inoculate" is off, any file that is backed up and has not been inoculated will create an alert. This may cause the backup program to time-out while waiting for the Virus Intercept alert.

Most popular backup programs (tape- or diskette-based) include some form of file compression. Virus Intercept will be unable to scan for viruses as compressed files are being restored (same problem as PKUNZIP). Be sure to check them with Virus Clinic for viruses.

Time-Sensitive Programs

Some programs may require a response from a device or connection within a specific time or the program will time-out, assuming the device has failed or the connection has been broken. On most computers, the normal operation of Virus Clinic should cause no problems. However, a virus alert may halt operation long enough for the communications program or backup program to experience a time-out fault.

Disk Copy

DOS's DISKCOPY command does not operate on a file-by-file basis. Therefore, Virus Intercept cannot scan for viruses during a DISKCOPY. Viewing a directory of the source disk prior to the DISKCOPY permits Virus Intercept to scan for boot-sector viruses. Virus Clinic is needed to scan for program-infector viruses.

High-Memory Managers

Virus Intercept will check programs for viruses as they are loaded into *high memory*. This check prevents a virus from hiding in high memory.

Virus Intercept itself can be loaded into high memory. It is important to know that if you are running QEMM or 386MAX, you must load the memory manager first. Also, be sure to check the READ.ME file for the latest information about using memory managers and NAV_.SYS.

Virus Intercept and Disk Compressors

Virus Intercept will work with most automatic hardware or software disk compressors, such as Stacker. If Norton AntiVirus is loaded on a compressed disk partition, before loading Virus Intercept, be sure to load the driver that enabled the compressed disk partition.

Boot-Sector Scan on Warm Boot

The warm-boot trap actually traps the Ctrl+Alt+Del keyboard sequence so that programs that emulate a warm boot, such as WARM.COM (a public-domain program), will bypass the boot-sector scan-feature of Virus Intercept. Virus Intercept also does not trap warm boots on XT-class or 8088-based PCs.

> **NOTE:** If you update Norton AntiVirus's virus definitions (see Chapter 7, "Updating Norton AntiVirus"), the new virus signatures do not go into effect with Virus Intercept until the next reboot.

Summary

Virus Intercept is your defensive line against viruses. The four versions provide varying levels of protection and performance. When Virus Intercept sounds a virus alarm, reboot and go on the offensive with Virus Clinic.

Using Virus Clinic

Virus Intercept watches in the background for any viral activity. *Virus Clinic* takes a more aggressive approach, actively searching for viruses and repairing or deleting infected files. Virus Clinic also serves as the controlling interface for other Norton AntiVirus functions, such as uninoculating files, maintaining virus definitions, and customizing Norton AntiVirus.

Virus Clinic can run interactively or can be executed in a command-line manner suitable for batch files. Virus Clinic is executed interactively by the C:\NAV> NAV command.

When Virus Clinic is first executed, it opens with a Scan Disk dialog box, ready to scan the entire default drive. Pressing Enter begins the virus scan. Press Esc to exit or back out of the dialog box (see figure 6-1).

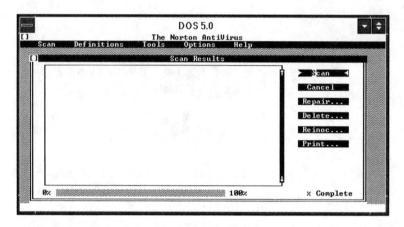

Figure 6-1 Virus Clinic opens, ready to scan the default drive

If a program-infecting virus is active or live in memory, it's likely that NAV.EXE will be infected when DOS opens NAV.EXE for execution. If this happens, Virus Clinic will inform you that NAV.EXE has been altered and may be infected. NAV.EXE then aborts back to the DOS prompt. You should assume that a virus is present and turn off the PC.

Navigating Virus Clinic

The DOS version of Virus Clinic, NAV.EXE, conforms to the Common User Access or CUA interface. All the Norton Utilities are now consistent with CUA. A good example of a CUA program is DOS 5.0's *Edit*. CUA programs are event-driven, which means *within limits*. You can select any program task at any time. A CUA program *responds* to events rather than forcing you through a series of menus or steps.

This method of control is more intuitive than earlier styles of interfaces. CUA also allows the DOS program to have a similar look and feel to its Windows counterpart. The following tables provide terms, definitions, and instructions for navigating through Virus Clinic.

Event Control	Function
Command button	Performs a function, such as executing a task, opening a dialog box, or canceling an action.
Check box	Toggles options on or off. Check boxes are used when several options can be set simultaneously.
List box	Displays a set of items, such as virus definitions, directories, or files.
Text box	Edits text information, such as a filename, virus definition, or password.
Pull-down menu	Displays tasks for selection and execution.

Key Combination	Action
Alt+*shortcut key* (Alt + the first letter of the menu item)	Opens a pull-down menu.
Arrow keys	Move the cursor to the nearest item Press the up- and down-arrow keys to move the cursor in a list box. Press the right- and left-arrow keys to move the cursor in a text box. Press the up- and down-arrow keys to move through the current menu, and press the right- and left-arrow keys to move to an adjacent menu.

continues

Key Combination	Action
End	Moves to the end or bottom of a list or text box.
Enter	Selects the current item in a menu, or completes a dialog box.
Esc (Escape)	Cancels the current dialog box or operation without further action and returns you to the previous screen.
F1	Pops up context-sensitive help menu.
Home	Moves to the beginning or top of a list or text box.
PageDown	Moves you down through a list box.
PageUp	Moves you up through a list box, one screen display at a time.
Shift+Tab	Counter rotates between items in a dialog box.
Shortcut key (red letter in menu item)	Selects an item from a pull-down menu.
Spacebar	Toggles the highlighted item between selected and not selected. A checkmark appears by the selected items. In some dialog boxes, the space bar executes the choice and closes the dialog box.
Tab	Rotates between items within a dialog box.

NOTE: When scrolling through a list box, selecting an item and pressing Enter does not choose that item. You must press the spacebar to select the item.

Press Tab to rotate to command buttons in dialog boxes. A dialog box often will default to the list object. Once the list choices are selected using the spacebar, you must highlight the OK button with the Tab key to actually act on your selection.

Navigating with the Mouse

Using a mouse is preferable with Virus Clinic. A reverse-color character box or a graphics arrow indicates the position of the mouse. The mouse can open menus, select items, slide scroll lists, and operate command buttons. Except for entering a filename, Virus Clinic can be operated easily solely by using the mouse.

If a mouse driver is active, Virus Clinic should make use of the mouse automatically. The mouse can be customized within Virus Clinic using the Video and Mouse Options command in the Options menu or with the NAVSETUP.EXE program.

Using Help

The on-line help provides a hypertext summary of the Norton AntiVirus manual. You can get on-line help the following two ways:

- The most useful method presents a context-sensitive help screen when you press F1. Help presents the instructional topic for the dialog box or menu item that is currently highlighted.

- The entire Help system can be viewed via the Help menu. The Help Index provides a complete list of the help topics in outline format (see figure 6-2). Selecting one of these topics presents the help text.

Several of the help texts offer more information about related topics. These topics, referred to as "See Also:," may be viewed in a hypertext fashion by selecting the GOTO command button at the bottom of the Help screen.

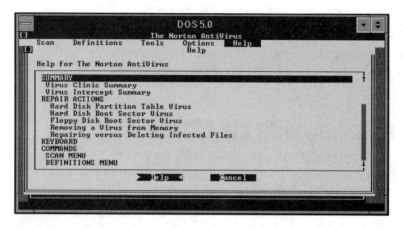

Figure 6-2 The Help Index

Virus Clinic's Menus

Following is a brief overview of Virus Clinic's menu structure:

Scan—Provides the main function of Virus Intercept: scanning for viruses on a drive or in a specified directory or individual file.

Definitions—Enables you to view or print a list of known viruses. Virus definitions can also be modified or updated.

Tools—Provides easy access to two Norton AntiVirus maintenance functions. As with RESCUE.EXE, Virus Clinic prepares rescue files containing the partition table, boot sector, and CMOS data, and restores the data in case of an emergency. A disk can be uninoculated by removing the checksum information for the drive.

Options—Presents a quick way to customize Virus Intercept and Virus Clinic.

Scanning for Viruses

Virus Clinic can search for a virus throughout an entire disk drive or perform a limited search on a directory or selected files. Note that Virus Clinic will scan the boot sector for viruses only while scanning an entire drive.

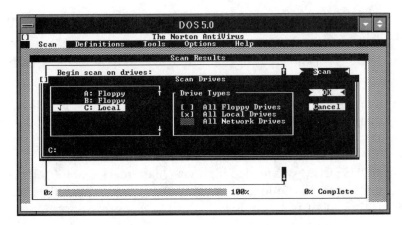

Figure 6-3 Scan Drives dialog box

Virus Clinic first scans memory to see if a virus is presently "live." Virus Clinic will scan *conventional memory* (0–640Kb) only once each time it is run. Subsequent virus scans will not rescan memory.

High Memory

```
┌───────────────────────  DOS 5.0  ──────────────────▼│▲│
│  Quarterdeck   ┌────────────────────────────────────────────┐
│  MANIFEST      │ Overview  Programs   Interrupts  BIOS Data   Timings │
│                ├────────────────────────────────────────────┤
│ ┌────────────┐ │                                            │
│ │   System   │ │  Memory Area   Size    Description         │
│ └────────────┘ │  0000 - 003F    1K     Interrupt Area      │
│ ► First Meg ◄  │  0040 - 004F   0.3K    BIOS Data Area       │
│ ┌────────────┐ │  0050 - 006F   0.5K    System Data          │
│ │  Expanded  │ │  0070 - 0B14   42K     DOS                  │
│ └────────────┘ │  0B15 - 20E8   87K     Program Area         │
│ ┌────────────┐ │  20E9 - 9FFF  508K     [Available]          │
│ │  Extended  │ │  ═══Conventional memory ends at 640K═══     │
│ └────────────┘ │  A000 - AFFF   64K     VGA Graphics         │
│ ┌────────────┐ │  B000 - B7FF   32K     Unused               │
│ │    DOS     │ │  B800 - BFFF   32K     VGA Text             │
│ └────────────┘ │  C000 - C7FF   32K     Video ROM            │
│ ┌────────────┐ │  C800 - CBFF   16K     Unused               │
│ │   Hints    │ │  CC00 - CFFF   16K     Mappable             │
│ └────────────┘ │  D000 - D3FF   16K     Unused               │
│ ┌────────────┐ │  D400 - DFFF   48K     Mappable             │
│ │    Exit    │ │                                            │
│ └────────────┘ │         Press PgDn for More                │
│ F1=Help F2=Print└────────────────────────────────────────────┘
└──────────────────────────────────────────────────────┘
```

Figure 6-4 Quarterdeck's MANIFEST displaying conventional and high memory usage

There is some controversy as to whether an antivirus scanner should scan high memory for the presence of a virus. Having examined the current state of virus technology, the Norton AntiVirus development team chose to limit the memory scan to DOS low memory. Following are the facts:

- There is no known virus that can load into high memory without the help of a memory manager's LOADHI command.

- If an infected program is loaded into high memory, it is likely that the virus will also load into high memory. We have personally observed the Jerusalem virus (the most common program-infecting virus) load into high memory when an infected MOUSE.COM was loaded high via Quarterdeck QEMM. All versions of Virus Clinic catch a virus attempting to load high, just as they identify a virus loading into DOS low memory.

- It is only possible for a program-infecting virus to load into high memory.

- A virus-infected Windows program will crash Windows. This keeps Windows from hiding a live virus in extended memory. During testing, Windows 3.1 crashed several times when a virus was introduced. If the virus is live when Windows 3.1 is loaded, C:\WIN31\SYSTEM\WIN386.EXE will likely be corrupted and will not load.

- As with any virus, if a virus is suspected to be live in high memory, disable the virus by turning off the computer. Then remove the virus from the infected file.

False Alarms

It's possible to receive false alarms identifying a virus that isn't there. Norton AntiVirus has been designed to operate as unobtrusively as possible, minimizing false alerts. However, it's possible for antivirus software to ring a false alarm when scanning the following:

- Another antivirus program. (The antivirus program may find the virus signatures stored in the data files of the other antivirus program. Norton AntiVirus encrypts its virus signatures so other antivirus programs should not report a virus when scanning NAV_.SYS.)

- Graphic images.

- Programs that regularly update their executable files.

If a virus is found in memory, Virus Clinic will halt the scan at the first sign of a live virus. It is unwise for any program to operate while a virus is live in memory. Program-infector viruses can infect more files as the files are read from the disk. If the scan is continued, Norton AntiVirus would be inviting the virus to infect every executable file that Virus Clinic scanned. (This is true for some viruses.)

What's worse, if the virus in memory is a stealth virus, Virus Clinic's scan for the viruses on the disk may be rendered inaccurate by the virus.

Scanning for viruses while the virus is live is fighting the virus while it is strongest. That would be akin to letting a military enemy choose the place and time of battle. The critical first step is to disarm the virus so it's not living in memory. To disarm the virus, follow these steps:

1. Turn off the computer. (Physically power off the computer.) Some viruses load outside of DOS's domain and may survive a warm boot (Ctrl+Alt+Del). The Alameda virus's main method of reproduction is to pretend to reboot in response to your warm boot, and then infect your clean boot disk.

2. Reboot from the Rescue Diskette you created in Chapter 5, "Getting Started with Norton AntiVirus." If you did not create a dedicated Rescue Diskette, reboot with a known clean copy of DOS. This keeps a boot sector virus or COMMAND.COM infecting virus from becoming live.

3. Run Virus Clinic (NAV.EXE) from the Rescue Diskette. If the Rescue Diskette is not available, run a known clean copy of Virus Clinic. The Virus Clinic loaded on the hard disk may have been infected or corrupted by the virus. As a protection, Virus Clinic carefully monitors its own file signature and will refuse to run if it is altered.

4. Scan the entire disk. If the virus is a boot-sector infector, the Virus Clinic disk scan will find it. If the virus is a program infector, an entire disk scan is recommended to locate every infected file. The following sections describe removing boot-sector viruses and infecting viruses.

If a Virus Is Found in the Boot Sector

Boot-sector viruses attach to the boot sector of a hard disk or diskette or they attach to the partition table of a hard disk. Every diskette or disk, whether it is a bootable disk, contains a small program in the first sector that loads DOS or displays an error if DOS is unavailable. It is this small program that boot-sector viruses infect. When an infected diskette is booted, regardless of whether it loads DOS, the virus becomes active and infects the hard disk.

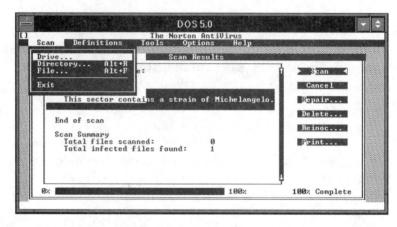

Figure 6-5 Having identified Michelangelo, Virus Clinic is ready to repair the boot sector

Boot-sector viruses load into memory before the PC even begins to search for a copy of DOS. Once DOS is loaded, the virus is already in memory, outside of DOS's memory limits. This makes it difficult for traditional antivirus software to detect live boot-sector viruses by searching memory. (Virus Clinic will find a boot-sector virus hiding below DOS.)

The decrease in DOS memory is also the boot-sector virus's dead giveaway. A simple CHKDSK or MEM command will show that a boot-sector virus is alive and stealing memory from DOS. The Michelangelo virus, for example, stole 2Kb from DOS, and the Total Available Memory reported by MEM went from 655,360 to 653,312.

Note that while this is usually true, a stealth virus could feed DOS false information, making it appear as if the 640Kb was intact.

Repairing a Boot-Sector Virus

Once the scan is complete, Virus Clinic will give you the option of repairing the boot sector and removing the virus. Highlight the boot-sector virus and press Tab to select the Repair command button. Virus Clinic will attempt to heal the boot sector automatically.

In most cases, Virus Clinic can remove the offending virus and repair the boot sector. Most boot-sector viruses make a copy of the original boot sector that can be restored. If however, after the virus is repaired, the computer fails to boot normally, there are three possible actions:

- An undocumented feature of MS DOS 5.0's FDISK has the capability to "freshen" the Master Boot Record or the executable portion of the partition table. The syntax is FDISK/MBR. In this mode, FDISK will not present the normal `create and delete disk partition menu` message, but will correct any problems with the partition table and quickly return to a DOS prompt. In some cases, boot-sector viruses have been removed with the FDISK /MBR command.

- Run Norton Disk Doctor (NDD.EXE) and Norton Disk Tools (DISKTOOL.EXE). These programs will analyze the system areas of the disk and attempt to make them bootable.

- The boot sector can be restored from the Rescue Diskette by the Rescue function of Virus Clinic or by RESCUE.EXE.

If all this fails to make the disk bootable, you have no choice but to repartition the disk. However, it is likely that Rescue has made the disk accessible so that you can create a current backup set. To do this, follow these steps:

1. Boot from the A: drive and attempt to access the C: drive.

2. Perform a complete backup.

3. Using FDISK, delete all the current partitions.

4. Using FDISK, create a new DOS partition.

5. Using FORMAT C: /S, format the disk with the system files.

6. You should now be able to boot from the hard disk.

7. Restore from your original program diskettes and data backup.

8. Scan the entire drive again using Virus Clinic.

> **NOTE:** A boot-sector virus can be removed from a diskette by copying the files to the hard disk and reformatting the diskette.

If a Virus Is Found in a File

Program-infector viruses attach to executable files and load as TSRs (memory-resident programs) when you run the infected program. While a virus is running as a TSR, it is referred to as a live virus. The virus remains alive until you reboot and remove the virus from memory. All the while, the virus is infecting every other program that DOS opens by executing or copying the file. If the virus has been on your PC for a while, it is probable that several, if not all, of the programs on your computer are infected.

Repairing Program-Infector Viruses

Once all of the infected programs and viruses are identified, Virus Clinic presents a dialog box. You can choose to repair the infected file and remove the virus, delete the infected file, or ignore the virus (see figure 6-6). Virus Clinic will only allow you to select repair for an infection that can be repaired.

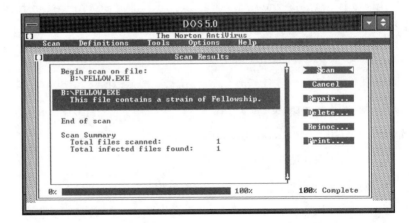

Figure 6-6 The 4096 (Frodo) virus can be removed from the infected file or the infected file can be deleted

Some viruses corrupt the file as they are infecting it. The files can no longer be repaired but must be deleted. In this case you'll have to restore the original files or reinstall the software package.

> **NOTE:** If the original file is available, you may want to compare the repaired file with the original as proof of a proper repair (use the DOS COMP command). In our testing, we found only one case where the repaired file was not a perfect match. The NAV Virus Detection Lab is constantly working to increase the number of virus infections that can be repaired.

Detecting Unknown Viruses

```
If you suspect an unknown virus,
do not pass go,
do not collect $200.
```

Immediately quarantine the infected PC.

Norton AntiVirus identifies unknown viruses, or more properly, viruses whose signatures have not yet been added to Norton AntiVirus's Virus Definition, by watching for virus-like symptoms and activities.

Be sure to check the hardware and software configuration before assuming you have a new virus. New virus strains are rare. Very rare. The odds are significantly stronger that you have a software conflict or a hardware failure.

Viruses tend to do certain things. An infected file will often grow in size or, even if the virus overwrote a part of the file, the file's checksum would change and it may no longer behave properly. A boot-sector virus will change the amount of total system memory as DOS reports it. By feeding DOS false information, stealth viruses may hide some of these clues to the casual observer. A new virus may not be found until it activates and you see a message or it attempts to damage your data.

A virus watcher's greatest fear is that a virus will remain undetected for several years as it spreads. If the virus writer was patient enough to wait five years for the activation, a vast majority of computers could be affected. The worst Michelangelo predictions would pale beside the destructive capabilities of a truly bug-free stealth virus that kept itself hidden for several years.

Fortunately, the tendency has been for viruses to be imperfect, and those flaws give the virus away. You may recall from Chapter 2 how the Jerusalem virus's reinfection of .EXE files alerted Israel to the virus before its activation date.

Virus Intercept's Comprehensive Scan, with Write Protect enabled (NAV_.SYS /W), will stop an unknown virus from doing significant damage to the system portion of your disk. However, it is still possible for individual files to be altered. Following are some "unknown virus" clues:

- Inoculation change.

- Change in Total System Memory as reported by CHKDSK, MEM, or Norton SYSINFO.

- Attempts to write to the boot sector.

- COMMAND.COM altered.

- Sudden degredation in performance.

- Strange software behavior.

- Message from the virus that appears on-screen.

Reporting a New Virus

Once you've reported an unknown virus, virus researchers will disassemble the virus to discern its signature and lineage, and to identify the virus's trigger and possible effect. Often, a new virus is in fact a variant of a known existing virus. The signature may have been changed to evade detection, or the trigger may have been changed (such as changing from Friday the 13th to Tuesday the 13th as in the Anarkia variant of the Jerusalem virus). The effect may have been changed, as in the case of the Cascade virus (which causes letters to fall to the bottom of the screen during the months of fall—a nuisance virus) that was altered to become the 1704 format virus, which formats the hard disk as the letters fall, but only during the months of fall.

It is important that the computing community is quickly notified of any new virus strains. Early detection will allow the antivirus industry to provide protection, which helps to stop the spread of the virus.

When reporting a virus, include a virus sample and all the documentation you can. You should call Symantec and Patricia Hoffman before sending the diskette. Patricia Hoffman has been accepted as the Antivirus Industry librarian. She officially identifies and catalogs virus strains.

The NAV Virus Detection Lab places a higher priority on viruses found in the field by customers than viruses reported by other researchers. If you report a new virus strain, the NAV Virus Detection Lab expects to identify the virus and respond with a new virus signature within 48 hours.

Some corporations may be cautious about letting the public know their computers were hit by rogue software. In this case, report the virus anonymously, but please report it.

Virus samples should be sent to the following organizations. Use a standard diskette mailer or make one out of cardboard.

Send samples to

>Virus Detection Lab
>NAV Tech Support Group
>Symantec/Peter Norton Group
>2500 Broadway Ave.
>Suite 200
>Santa Monica, CA 90404

>(310) 441-4900

or

>Patricia M. Hoffman
>3333 Bowers Ave Suite 130
>Santa Clara, CA 95054

>(408) 988-3773

You should also notify

- The suspected source of the virus.

- Any other users to whom you may have passed on the virus unknowingly.

- Your corporate Information Services Dept., PC Information Center, or Micro Manager.

- The local computer service center you patronize (to inform them of the risk in the area).

- The SysOps of any BBSes where you may have unknowingly uploaded infected files.

Documenting the Virus

To fully document the attack, the following several factors must be included:

- Your system configuration, including hardware, DOS version, AUTOEXEC.BAT, CONFIG.SYS, and memory configuration.

- Every symptom that alerted you to the presence of a virus, such as affected performance or messages.

- Any damage that was inflicted by the virus. (Explain exactly what happened to the disk drive.)

- Any steps you took (successful or unsuccessful) to remove the virus.

- The suspected source and method of transmission.

Collecting a Sample

To collect a sample of an unknown boot-sector virus, follow these steps to ensure that the virus infects the diskette:

1. FORMAT A: /S.

   This will copy the system files and COMMAND.COM to the diskette. If possible use a 5 1/4-inch diskette. Some viruses will not infect a 3 1/2-inch diskette.

2. DIR A:

   Accesses the diskette drive and gives the virus another chance to infect the diskette.

3. Write-protect the diskette.

4. Clearly label the diskette as virus-infected.

To collect a sample of an unknown program-infecting virus, follow these steps:

1. FORMAT A: /S

   This replicates your system for the virus testers and copies COMMAND.COM (some viruses only infect COMMAND.COM).

2. Copy all the files suspected to be infected to the diskette.

   Most likely, the infected files include the program that was being executed when the virus struck and any other program that has seen a checksum change.

3. Write-protect the diskette.

4. Clearly label the diskette as virus-infected.

5. Once the sample has been sent to the virus research labs, destroy every copy of the virus!

It is not safe to maintain a private virus library. The risk of accidental reinfection and the liability when the virus spreads are too great. Unless very strict containment measures are followed, it is likely that the virus would spread again.

Several virus fighters we interviewed while preparing for this book said their biggest problem with virus infections was a reinfection a few weeks after they completely cleaned their client's computers of the virus infection. Invariably, someone had an infected diskette at home, or an infected diskette was in a drawer during the virus cleaning.

Keep in mind that if the virus is a new virus strain, you can never be sure that you have already seen the virus's total damage.

Restoring the Infected PC

Because the virus has not yet been identified by the Norton Virus Detection Lab, repairing the infected files is impractical. Using debug or the Norton Utilities Disk Editor, it is theoretically possible to return the file to its original state. However, deleting the infected file and restoring from a known clean source is recommended.

> **NOTE:** Please, before you delete the virus and restore, make a sample and at least notify Symantec and Patricia Hoffman.

Recovering with Rescue

If the virus attack caused the PC to be unable to boot, it's likely that the partition table or boot sector were damaged. Before performing a low-level format and repartitioning the disk, it's worthwhile to attempt to restore the original information using the Norton AntiVirus Rescue feature (see figure 6-7). Rescue saves or restores the critical system information necessary for a disk to be bootable.

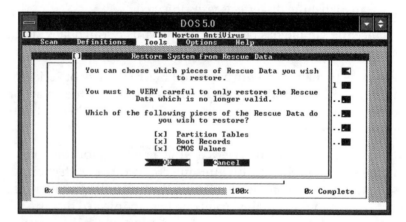

Figure 6-7 Restore Rescue Data selections

Partition Table, Boot Sector, and CMOS Information

The *partition table* is the first physical sector of the hard disk. It contains information about the partitioning of the disk drive. For example, a 212Mb drive may be partitioned as two 106Mb drives. Prior to DOS 3.1, each disk partition was limited to 32Mb. Therefore, a typical 40Mb drive was often partitioned as a 20Mb C: drive and a 20Mb D: drive.

The partition table also contains a small program called the *Master Boot Record* that finds the bootable disk partition and runs its boot sector. Note that diskettes cannot be partitioned and do not have partition tables.

The first sector of every diskette and disk partition contains a small program that locates and finds DOS or displays a message stating the disk or diskette is not a bootable disk. This first sector and its small program is called the *boot sector*.

The *CMOS* (Complementary Metal-Oxide Semiconductor) holds the hardware setup information. Information about the computer system board, memory size, diskette types, hard disks type, sector size, date and time, and other advanced features such as shadow RAM and memory caching is contained in the CMOS. Most PCs are built with a CMOS editor in ROM, allowing modification of the CMOS Setup during the boot sequence (for example: `Press <ESC> to run Set-Up`).

Restoring the Rescue Files

RESCUE.EXE recommends that you should only attempt to restore the rescue file after first attempting to correct the problems with Norton Disk Doctor.

1. Boot the computer from the Rescue Diskette you created. If a Rescue Diskette is unavailable, boot with a known clean copy of DOS.

2. Run Rescue.

3. Run NAV.EXE.

   Select Restore from Rescue Disk from the Tools menu; run Norton AntiVirus's RESCUE.EXE Program (select Restore from the Rescue Diskette); run the RESCUE /RESTORE; or run Norton Utilities' DISKTOOL.EXE. (Select Restore from the Rescue Diskette.)

4. Follow the dialog boxes to select the appropriate Rescue data files and restore the data.

5. Reboot to test the restored configuration.

If the PC still will not boot, run Norton Disk Doctor on the restored configuration; run FDISK /MBR to freshen the partition table; or call Symantec Tech Support at (310) 441-4900.

6. If you are still unable to boot from the hard disk drive, you have no choice but to repartition the disk. It is likely that Rescue has made the disk accessible so that you can now create a current backup set.

To repartition the hard disk drive, follow these steps:

1. Boot from the A: drive and attempt to access the C: drive.

2. Using Virus Clinic, scan the entire C: drive, deleting infected files.

3. Back up any data files you want to save. Do not back up any programs—they are probably infected.

4. Using FDISK, delete all the current partitions.

5. Using FDISK, create a new DOS partition.

6. Using FORMAT C: /S, format the disk with the system files.

7. You should now be able to boot your computer from the hard disk.

8. Restore from your original program diskettes and data backup.

9. Rescan the entire drive using Virus Clinic.

NOTE: To restore the partition table, boot sector, or CMOS, you must have saved the information previously with the Rescue-Save Data command. Also, Rescue will not run properly in a multitasking environment. Do not run Rescue under Windows or DESQview.

Configuring Virus Clinic

In the Options menu of Virus Clinic, the Clinic selection lets you tailor Virus Clinic to your preferences (see figure 6-8). The commands presented at the completion of a scan can be individually enabled.

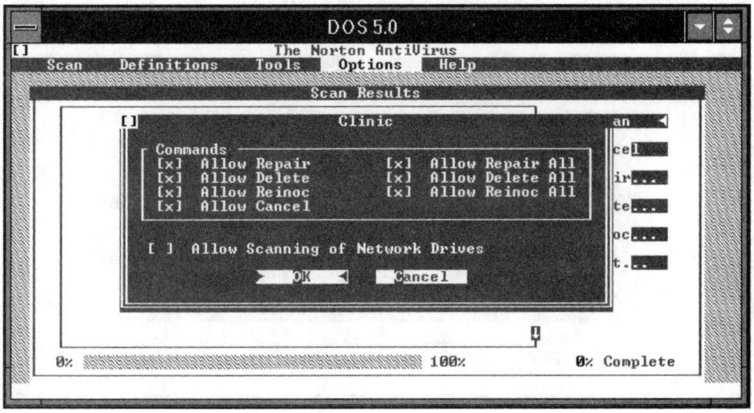

Figure 6-8 Virus Clinic configuration options

Allow Repair (All) repairs the infected files. Repair may not be possible with some viral infections. The Repair All command repairs all the infected files that were detected as opposed to repairing them individually.

Allow Delete (All) deletes the infected files. Deleting the infected files always removes the virus; however, the program must be restored or reinstalled.

Allow Reinoc (All) reinoculates the file if the file signature has changed due to normal program operation.

Allow Cancel permits canceling the scan.

Allow Scanning of Network Drives enables you to scan only local drives.

Global Options

The Global Options determine how both Virus Clinic and Virus Intercept behave (see figure 6-9).

Figure 6-9 The Global Options dialog box

If Detect Unknown Viruses is checked, Norton AntiVirus will inoculate all executable files and monitor their file signatures. Any unexplained change in the file signature indicates the possibility of an unknown virus.

Auto-inoculating files means that you will not be alerted the first time Norton AntiVirus finds a new program file. Note that this option does not reinoculate without your approval.

If your programs include executable code in nonstandard files (other than *.EXE, *.COM, *.BAT, *.OVL, *.SYS, *.DLL), you should disable Scan Executables Only. Note that this takes significantly longer than scanning just executables.

The Network Inoculation Directory enables you to specify the location of the inoculation file for the network drives, and the Custom Message enables you to display your own warning message during virus alerts.

Command Line Control

Virus Clinic may be also be executed at the command line level. In this mode, it simply scans and reports any viruses. NAV.EXE can also be used to pass configuration preferences to Virus Clinic.

Following are the command line options:

```
C:\NAV>Norton AntiVirus /?

The Norton AntiVirus, 2.0, Copyright 1989-1991 by
Symantec Corporation


Find and remove viruses in files, directories, and
drives.


NAV [/A]¦[pathname... [/S][/REFRESH]]
NAV [/SOUND[+¦-]] [/BOX[+¦-]] [/PRESENCE]


pathname              Any valid drive, directory, or
                      file name.

A                     Scan all drives.

BOX                   Enable/disable the intercept
                      visible alert.

PRESENCE              A compatible Intercept is present
                      in RAM.

S                     Scan subdirectories of any
                      directory named.

REFRESH               Inoculate or reinoculate all
                      files scanned.

SOUND                 Enable/disable the intercept
                      audible alarm.


C:\NAV>
```

Launch Virus Clinic and Scan for Viruses

NAV.EXE, followed by the switch /A, drive designation, directory, or filename, will launch Virus Clinic and begin scanning for viruses. Just as in the interactive mode, NAV.EXE will first scan memory, and then scan any drive or directory specified in the parameters. Optionally, the scan can update the checksum records for executable files.

You also may direct Virus Intercept to turn on or off the Virus alert sound or virus alert boxes using NAV.EXE /BOX+ /SOUND-, as in the following examples:

C:\>NAV /A /S	Scans all subdirectories of all drives.
C:\>NAV \Procomm\download	Scans the subdirectory used to collect downloaded software.
C:\>NAV /BOX+ /SOUND-	Turns on the virus alert boxes without the sound.
C:\>NAV /S /REFRESH	Scans all the directories of C:, reinoculating the files as it goes.
C:\>NAV \COMMAND.COM	Scans COMMAND.COM only.

ErrorLevels Returned

DOS permits a program to set the DOS ErrorLevel variable depending on its success. ErrorLevel can be included in DOS batch commands to direct the logical flow of the batch file.

ErrorLevel	Meaning
1	Virus found in memory
2	Virus Clinic may be infected
3	Viruses detected during scan
4	No viruses detected
5	Device Driver is not active in RAM
6	Device Driver is active in RAM
255	Scan not completed

You can use NAV.EXE in batch files and it will return an ErrorLevel so that you can handle the results. For example, you may want to scan COMMAND.COM every time you boot. This has the added benefit of finding any boot-sector viruses that loaded into memory prior to Virus Intercept. The following demonstrates how a batch file can branch depending on NAV.EXE's ErrorLevel.

```
AUTOEXEC.BAT
@ECHO OFF
C:\NAV\NAV /COMMAND.COM
IF ERRORLEVEL = 1 GOTO BSVIRUS
IF ERRORLEVEL = 2 GOTO COMVIRUS
(other AUTOEXEC.BAT commands)
GOTO END
:BSVIRUS
ECHO Warning: NAV found a virus in memory!
GOTO END
:COMVIRUS
ECHO Warning: COMMAND.COM infected!
:END
```

Summary

Virus Clinic is the part of Norton AntiVirus that gets the job done. It scans for viruses and removes them or deletes the infected file.

Some viruses simply replicate without any effect. Other viruses display annoying messages or graphics. Variations of some of the merely annoying viruses do cause severe damage once they activate. The bottom line is that you can never trust a virus. The only good virus is a dead virus.

Different virus types require varying means of repair. Virus Clinic can sometimes remove program-infecting viruses. However, some viruses make this impossible. Boot-sector viruses infect the executable program that boots DOS and can usually be repaired.

A virus spreads fastest while it is unknown. To an unprotected computer, all viruses are effectively unknown. Once the virus research labs have identified the virus and the virus-fighting industry provides protection, the computing community can contain the spread of the virus. It is critical that new viruses are quickly reported.

Virus Clinic serves other functions beside scanning for viruses. It updates the virus definitions, uninoculates files, and reconfigures Norton AntiVirus. Virus Clinic can also be executed in a non-interactive manner suitable for batch files.

Advanced Norton AntiVirus

This last section presents three key elements of Norton AntiVirus. It's critical that any antivirus utility be kept up to date and able to detect new viruses. Norton AntiVirus goes to great lengths to keep you updated and protected.

With the growing popularity of MS-Windows and Norton Desktop for Windows, it's important that your antivirus utility is completely compatible with Windows. Norton AntiVirus with Norton Desktop for Windows goes beyond compatibility and makes virus fighting within Windows convenient.

An unprotected LAN is wide open for a virus infection. Once a few key program files become infected, the virus rapidly spreads. The combination of infected files on the file server and on local hard drives makes fighting a virus on a LAN very frustrating. Chapter 9 covers fighting viruses in a networked environment and includes important tips for keeping a LAN virus-free.

Updating Norton AntiVirus

Norton AntiVirus provides protection against tomorrow's virus in two ways. Norton AntiVirus maintains file signatures that identify virus activity, even from an unknown virus, and the NAV Virus Identification Lab keeps you updated with new virus signatures as they become available.

This chapter covers updating your copy of Norton AntiVirus with new virus signatures.

The Virus Signature List

Norton AntiVirus identifies viruses by using *virus signatures*. The signature tells Virus Intercept and Virus Clinic where to look in an infected file for tell-tale signs of the virus. The virus signature is also used by Virus Clinic to repair the infected file.

Sometimes, a single virus signature can be used to identify several individual virus strains of the same virus family. You may recall from the discussion on virus names in Chapter 2, the antivirus industry is currently in chaos over virus names. Different vendors use different naming schemes and most viruses have at least one alias. Widely spread viruses may have 15 to 20 alternate names. The NAV Virus Identification Lab tries to use the most common name, usually the one reported by Patricia Hoffman in her VSUM virus information summary.

New virus signatures not only provide protection against a newly identified virus—they also provide improved file-repair capabilities for known viruses.

Staying Current with Symantec/Peter Norton

The NAV Virus Identification Lab technicians want you to have their latest virus signatures. They go to extreme lengths to make the definitions conveniently available to you. Contact information for all of the following services is in your Norton AntiVirus documentation.

The Virus NewsLine

The Virus NewsLine is an automated voice newsletter that provides updated information about viruses and Norton AntiVirus. From a touchtone phone, you can also select solutions to common problems. Other than any long distance toll charges, the Virus NewsLine is a free service.

The *Symantec BBS* is a free service that has a file area with virus-related files and a Norton AntiVirus SIG. New virus definitions are posted on the Symantec BBS as soon as they are available. This BBS is also a great way to discuss any problems with Norton Technical Support.

Set your communication software to no parity, 8 data bits, and one stop bit.

CompuServe

Once you have logged in CompuServe, you can find lively discussions about viruses and using Norton AntiVirus by scrolling through the list of software forums or by entering GO NORUTL. The Norton Utilities Forum has several file and message sections. The NAV-IBM section contains files from Symantec/Peter Norton Group and message threads between users and Norton Technical Support.

The most common method of navigating CompuServe is CIM.EXE, which is available from CompuServe. The menu-driven communications program makes it easy to find files and follow discussion threads. To download new virus signatures using CIM, follow these steps:

1. Under the Services menu, type GO NORUTL.

2. CIM logs you into CompuServe automatically.

3. From the Library menu, select Browse Files.

4. Select the NAV-IBM library section.

5. Look for any files ending with the .DEF file extension. Norton Technical Support uses this extension to identify a virus definition file. A text file (*.TXT) with detailed instructions will usually accompany the definition file (see figure 7-1).

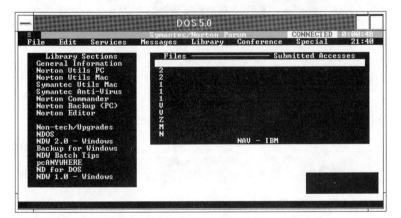

Figure 7-1 Selecting the Virus Signature Update in CompuServe

6. Double-click the definition file. CIM pops up a File Action dialog box. The box lets you view more information about the file, mark the file for download at a later time, or download the file immediately (see figure 7-2).

Figure 7-2 The File Action dialog box showing file information

7. Selecting Retrieve downloads the file to the directory of your choice automatically (see figure 7-3).

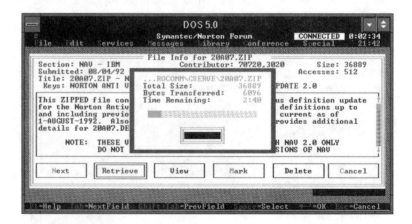

Figure 7-3 Downloading a virus definition file

NOTE: If you are not a CompuServe member and want to find out more about CompuServe, call (800) 848-8990.

Virus FaxLine

To make updating Norton AntiVirus as convenient as possible, Symantec also provides a *Virus FaxLine*. With a touchtone phone or a fax (be ready to receive), you can call the FaxLine and request that the most recent virus signatures be faxed to you automatically. The Virus FaxLine will make three attempts (10 minutes apart) to send you the fax. The fax contains the data required to enter the new virus signatures manually.

NOTE: Symantec will alternately mail you an update diskette if the other free methods are not convenient for you or you want to be absolutely sure you don't forget to check the free services for new virus signatures. The diskettes normally are sent out quarterly at a cost of $12.00 plus shipping, handling, and taxes. To order the update diskette service, call (800) 343-4714 extension 756.

Modifying the Virus Signature List

The Virus Signature List is maintained through Virus Clinic's Definitions Menu. "Load from File" is an easy way to update your virus signatures quickly from a downloaded file. The File Load dialog box lets you select the file containing the new virus signatures. Once you have selected the file, the virus signatures are loaded automatically. New virus signatures become available to Virus Intercept once you have rebooted.

Modify List—Presents a range of manual maintenance options.

Add—Enables you to enter new virus signatures manually. If you received the update via the Virus FaxLine or directly from Norton Tech Support, this method would be used to add the virus signature to Norton AntiVirus.

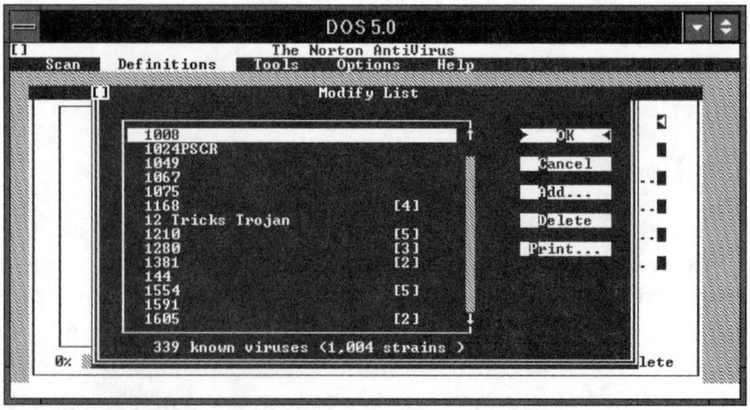

Figure 7-4 The Modify Virus dialog box

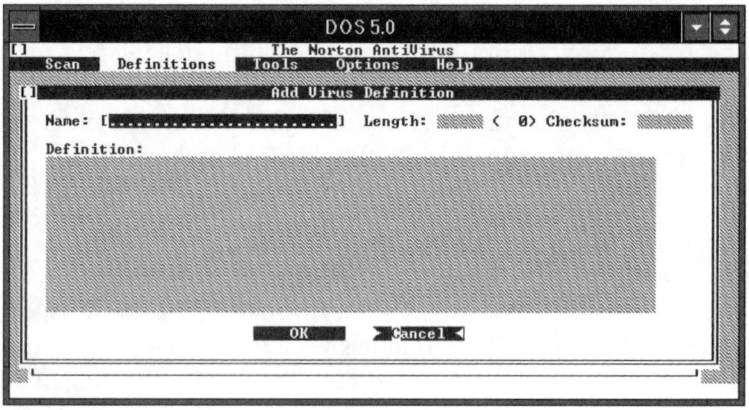

Figure 7-5 Manually adding a virus signature

Delete—Removes a virus signature from Norton AntiVirus's list of known viruses.

Print—Prints the list of known viruses to your printer or to a file.

Summary

New virus definitions are made available through many distribution methods. The update can be downloaded from a number of BBSes, including the Symantec BBS and CompuServe. Alternately, you can obtain the new virus definitions via your fax machine, or an update diskette can be mailed to you.

Updating Norton AntiVirus is easy. If you downloaded an update file, the Load From File command posts the new virus definitions into your NAV_.SYS file automatically. Manually, the virus definitions may be added by entering the virus information through the Add Virus Definitions dialog box.

Norton AntiVirus's capability to be updated quickly and easily means that you can be protected from new virus strains without waiting for a new version of an antivirus utility.

Using Norton AntiVirus with Windows

Viruses don't mix well with Windows.

If a program-infecting virus is live in memory when Windows is loaded, chances are that Windows will refuse to run. First, WIN.COM becomes infected as it loads. When Windows 3.1 Enhanced mode loads WIN386.EXE and it becomes infected, WIN386.EXE reports that it has become corrupted. You will need to reinstall Windows after the virus is removed.

Following are two other general cases where MS-Windows may encounter a virus:

- While in Windows, if you run an infected DOS program, Windows will load the virus as a memory-resident program available for that DOS window. While running, the virus will attempt to infect other programs and Windows may become corrupted. You also may meet with problems when you attempt to close the DOS window.

- During our testing, while running an infected program in Windows, Windows usually generated a `General Protection Fault` message due to the corrupted Windows header in the infected Windows program. The launching program (Norton Desktop or Program Manager) needed to be closed and Dr. Watson (Windows 3.1 diagnostic tool) logged the error.

One other key point about viruses and Windows: to display a program icon, Program Manager or Norton Desktop must open and read the executable file. This means a live virus would have a chance to infect every Windows program. It also means that Virus Intercept has a chance to scan all Windows programs as Windows is started.

Using Virus Intercept with Windows

As you may recall, Chapter 5 lists four versions of Virus Intercept. Besides the varying levels of protection, the different versions also provide different levels of Windows support.

Virus Intercept	Memory	Loading Windows	Execute Infected DOS Program	Execute Infected Windows Program
NAV&.SYS	1Kb	Unable to establish connection	DOS Box Alert	General Protection Fault
NAV&.SYS /B	6Kb		DOS Box Alert	General Protection Fault
NAV_.SYS	39Kb		Windows Dialog box	Windows Dialog Box
NAV_.SYS /W	39Kb		Windows Dialog Box	Windows Dialog Box

NAV_.SYS is the Virus Intercept version that provides the best Windows support. This version supports full Windows dialog boxes and detection of virus-infected Windows programs before the virus can cause an error in Windows.

Note that if you use an 8514a type video adapter, you may encounter some problems when NAVPOPUP.EXE attempts to display the Windows dialog box. An easy way to test your system is to format a diskette while NAV_.SYS /W is running. You should get a boot-sector Write Protection alert dialog box.

The NAVPOPUP icon can be hidden. The option is presented in the Windows Virus Clinic Options menu-Intercept-selection dialog box (see figure 8-1).

Figure 8-1 The Virus Intercept (NAVPOPUP) icon

Using Virus Clinic with Windows

Virus Clinic for Windows is a near clone of its DOS counterpart. The dialog boxes and menus functionally are the same. One difference is that you cannot create a rescue diskette or restore from the rescue files while in Windows.

Just as with the DOS version, Virus Clinic for Windows can repair or delete any infected files it detects (see figure 8-2).

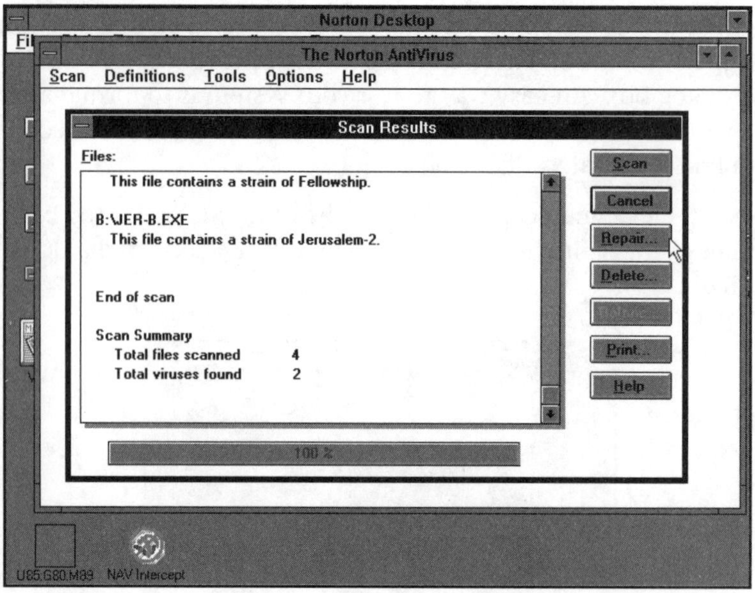

Figure 8-2 The file scan complete, Virus Clinic is ready to repair or delete the infected file

Norton Desktop for Windows

Norton AntiVirus is a seamless part of Norton Desktop for Windows. Norton Desktop provides several ways to launch Norton AntiVirus.

You can drag files with your mouse to the Norton AntiVirus *desktop agent*. Dropping them on that icon will launch a Virus Clinic scan of those files (see figure 8-3).

Following is a description of how to launch a Virus Clinic scan of particular files.

1. Open a drive window and select the file you want to scan. If you want to select more than one file, use the right mouse button to highlight nonsequential files. Pressing and holding down the right mouse button also highlights a continuous block of files.

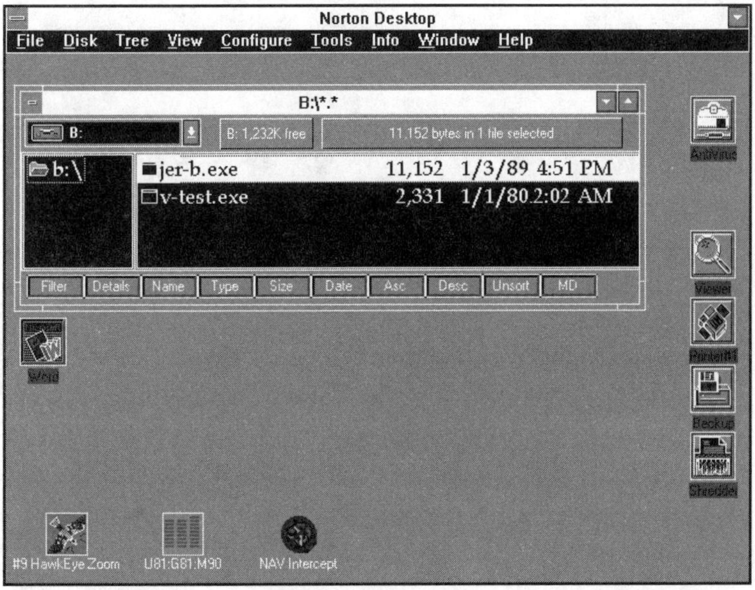

Figure 8-3 A Norton Disk View of two infected files. Dragging the files to the AntiVirus icon launches a Virus Clinic scan of the files.

2. While holding down the left mouse button, drag the files to the Norton AntiVirus desktop-agent icon. By default, the desktop agents are on the right side of the screen.

3. The Norton Scheduler can automatically run Virus Clinic to scan on a daily basis. This can be performed as a background task (similar to Norton Backup) or after hours.

Double-clicking on the Norton AntiVirus desktop agent will launch Virus Clinic. As with the DOS version of Virus Clinic, the program will open, ready to perform a scan on the default drive.

You can toggle on or off the Norton AntiVirus desktop agent in the Preferences dialog box found under the Norton Desktop's Configuration menu (see figure 8-4).

Another way that Norton Desktop offers to run Norton AntiVirus is if you have elected not to use Norton AntiVirus as a desktop agent, it is still available from the Tools menu (see figure 8-5).

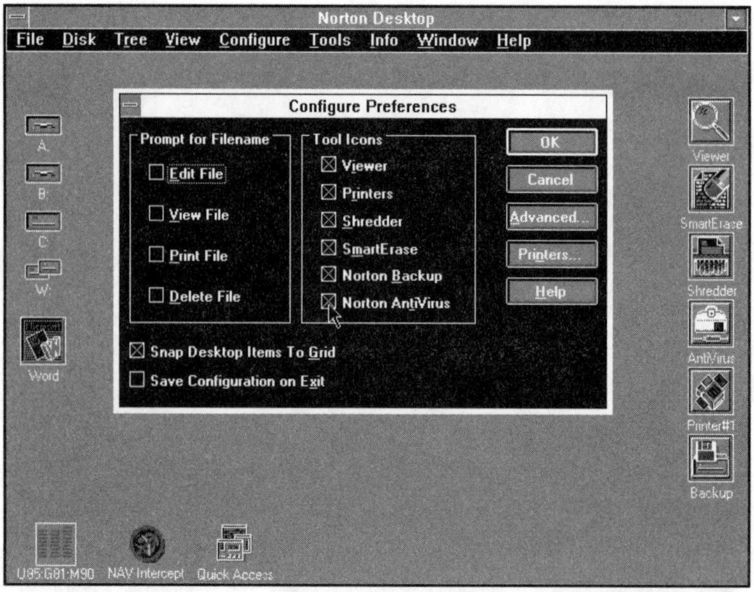

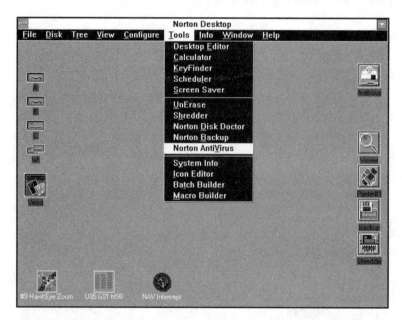

Figure 8-4 Norton Desktop for Windows Preferences with the Norton AntiVirus option

Figure 8-5 Norton Desktop's Tools menu provides access to Norton AntiVirus

Configuration Tips for Smooth Sailing in Windows 3.1

Following are some configuration tips that will enable Windows to run smoothly:

- Avoid QEMM stealth mode. It has been known to conflict with Norton AntiVirus.

- Check the Norton AntiVirus READ.ME file for the latest information about compatibility with Windows and memory managers.

- Be sure to keep NAVPOPUP.EXE in your load= line of WIN.INI. The Install program will place it there for you automatically.

- If you see the error `Unable to establish a link with NAV_.SYS` when Windows loads and you are running both Virus Intercept and NAVPOPUP.EXE, there may be a conflict between NAVPOPUP and another Windows program. If for example, AfterDark Version 1 caused this error, remove any other programs from the load= line in WIN.INI to help find the conflict.

Summary

Windows is fun, but a virus can wreak havoc in a Windows environment. Norton AntiVirus protects your computer while you are running Windows. If you also use Norton Desktop for Windows, the Norton AntiVirus seamlessly is added to the Desktop environment allowing you to drag and drop files onto Virus Clinic.

Virus Intercept also supports Windows and displays virus alerts in Windows dialog boxes.

Fighting Viruses on a LAN

The information lifeblood of most corporations is its *Local Area Network* or *LAN*. The threat of a virus running rampant on the LAN is a scary prospect. Because several users can share common files as well as these users often having their own local hard disks, disinfecting a LAN can be a frustrating experience.

All is not grim however. The improved file security and file monitoring available with a LAN can also aid in fighting viruses. This chapter explains how viruses behave on LANs, how to protect a LAN, and offers some tips on disinfecting a LAN.

Most of this chapter references *Novell Netware LANs*; however, you can apply these principles to other network operating systems as well.

How Viruses Behave on a LAN

A virus can spread like wildfire on a poorly administered LAN. Once key executable programs on the fileserver are infected, the virus can quickly infect every other program on every PC connected to the LAN.

It is possible to configure the LAN to contain the spread of a virus. For the "wildfire" example, we will assume the LAN has not been managed properly.

Program-Infector Viruses

A virus can spread on an unsecured LAN very quickly and easily. Following is a list of how a virus can spread like wildfire (see figure 9-1).

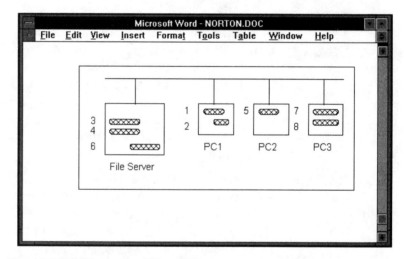

Figure 9-1 A Virus can spread like wildfire on an unsecured LAN

1. A program-infecting virus infects a program on the local hard disk of PC1. This infection happens in the same way the program-infecting viruses usually infect programs.

2. As PC1 executes other programs on its local hard drive, these other programs also become infected.

3. PC1 now logs onto the network and executes a program off the network fileserver. The fileserver program is now infected.

4. If the user runs a second program from the fileserver, that second program also becomes infected.

5. As more users log on the fileserver, the virus spreads to infect programs on those other local hard drives.

6. As the virus spreads, it is exposed to a growing number of other programs, which also become infected.

If the virus is one that reinfects infected programs, the file sizes of the infected programs will continue to grow as the files are reinfected. On a busy LAN, key programs may grow with such speed that within the day they are no longer executable.

Boot-Sector Viruses on a LAN

Boot-sector viruses actually spread more slowly on LAN environments. The virus cannot spread through the LAN to the fileserver or to other computers. The capability of the LAN to share data files means that there is less *sneaker-net* (the passing of diskettes to share information) so that diskettes that are infected with the boot-sector virus don't spread the virus as they would in a non-LAN environment.

The only way a fileserver can become infected with a boot-sector virus is to actually boot the fileserver from an infected diskette. A good safety measure is to build a clean network boot diskette, keep it by the fileserver and boot only from this diskette.

Novell Specific Viruses

There are two viruses that specifically target Novell Netware. According to a Novell Research Application Note's white paper, neither of the viruses have been reported "in the wild" as of March 1992.

The *Get Password 1* virus is a new strain of the Jerusalem virus designed to capture Netware login names and passwords and send the login information to a companion program also running somewhere on the network. Patricia Hoffman's *Virus Information Summary List* reports that "this code does not function properly and so there is no threat." Netware's encrypted passwords would render the virus impotent even if the virus successfully collected login information.

CZ2986, the second Netware virus, will load into the workstation memory and intercept logins. It will store up to 15 usernames and passwords in each infected file. While this Netware virus will collect passwords, a *cracker* (a cyberpunk who is attempting to break into your LAN) must know which files are infected, have rights to those files, and must inspect the files manually to extract the passwords. Prohibiting write operations to the infected files will stop this virus.

Fighting Viruses on a LAN

The basic philosophy of fighting viruses on a LAN is the same as fighting virus on a single computer. The primary differences are the connectivity that allows the virus to spread more rapidly and the increased security that can prevent a virus from writing to a program file. Following are the key concepts:

- Stop the virus as it attempts to become live in memory.

- If a virus is detected, remove the virus from memory by rebooting from a clean DOS diskette. The virus will then be at its weakest when you remove it.

- Just as you should isolate infected stand-alone computers, isolate the LAN components if a virus is detected on the LAN. This stops the virus from spreading while you clean the LAN.

The Client-Server Environment

A *client-server* LAN consists of several PCs (clients) that use the services of other computers (servers) dedicated to the task of providing the service to the client PCs. Fileservers provide high performance of shared files and control the access to those files. Although fileservers are the most common type of server, servers can provide any one of a number of specialized services, including database, mail, print, communication or fax, batch processing, or off-line storage, such as tape backup or CD-ROM access.

When a virus infects a single computer, the virus spreads within that computer during file open DOS requests. On a client-server LAN, the client PC requests the program file from the server computer. There is no way the virus can go from the client computer to the memory of the server computer. Even if the client computer is infected and the virus is active in memory, the server computer still retains control of the files on its own hard disk.

Client-server LANs generally provide a high level of reliability, performance, and security. Because the servers are dedicated to their service task, a server does not risk a user-application program crashing the server or limiting its performance.

Tips for Preventing Viral Infections on a Netware LAN

Following are some tips on how to prevent viruses from infecting Netware local area networks:

- Use diskless workstations wherever possible. This limits the introduction of viruses.

- Document the LAN. You should be able to find every computer, modem, and local drive in an emergency.

- Use call-back modems to protect against "crackers" and cyberpunks.

- Be especially careful when creating the DOSGEN for remote booting of diskless PCs. Be sure to scan every file before combining them with DOSGEN.

- Implement a Norton AntiVirus site license.

- Use NAV&.SYS on LAN diskless workstations to save memory.

- Regularly scan all volumes with Virus Clinic.

- Use Netware Groups to make user setups easier. This promotes the correct use of directory rights.

- Set as many read-only executable files as possible.

- Limit physical access to the fileserver.

- Be careful with supervisor access. No one should regularly login as the supervisor, nor should anyone be granted supervisor equivalent status. You may login as supervisor to perform supervisor functions, but then login as yourself when using the LAN regularly.

- Encourage good passwords—no dictionary words or names.

- Backup with a good automated backup system.

Recovering from a Virus Attack

If you detect a virus on your LAN, it can be very frustrating to track and destroy every copy of the virus. We designed these steps to assist you and assume that you are the LAN administrator and are familiar with Novell Netware.

We won't lie and tell you this will be fun—these tasks are time consuming and tedious. However, it is important that you, the LAN administrator(s), personally purge your LAN.

1. At the first sign of a possible virus, broadcast to all users that the server is going down immediately for corrective maintenance.

2. Log everyone off the fileserver, including yourself.

3. Lock out all users from the infected server.

4. Boot the LAN administrator's PC from a known clean diskette of DOS and run Norton AntiVirus Virus Clinic to remove any viruses from this PC.

5. From the just cleaned LAN administrator's PC, log on the server as system administrator and scan all executable files on all volumes of the server. Only execute programs from your local drive!

6. Repair or delete any viruses found. You may decide to reinstall programs that have been reinfected numerous times.

7. Starting with the most mission-critical computers, completely scan their local hard disks and all their diskettes. If you are being pressured by LAN users, you may elect to allow a few critical

"clean" computers to log back on the LAN. However, to avoid confusion, it is better if you can keep everyone off the server until you have certified the entire site virus-free.

Fighting Viruses on a Peer-to-Peer LAN

A *peer-to-peer network,* such as Artisoft's LANtastic, does not depend on a computer dedicated to providing a service. Instead, each computer on the LAN can be configured as a workstation, server, or both. A peer-to-peer LAN is well suited to a small office environment that needs to share files and printer resources.

In a peer-to-peer network, it is common for several users to have access to several hard drives. The smaller, "cozier" environment of a peer-to-peer LAN also means that most peer-to-peer LANS have not implemented the LAN's file or user security features. These two factors combined make viruses spread very quickly on peer-to-peer LANs.

Another difference between peer-to-peer LANs and client-server LANs is that a peer-to-peer LAN uses a regular DOS hard disk format and is susceptible to boot-sector viruses. The hard disk's DOS format also means that files can be repaired with standard DOS utilities.

Do not run Virus Intercept on a computer that is configured as a Lantastic server. A conflict between Virus Intercept and Lantastic may result in corrupted files. We recommend that Virus Intercept be run only at the individual workstations and that you regularly scan LANtastic servers with Virus Clinic.

If a peer-to-peer network becomes infected with a virus, the network should be shutdown. You should scan every computer and remove any viruses detected before you bring the LAN back into operation.

Configuring Norton AntiVirus for Multiple Users

We recommend the following Norton AntiVirus Configuration for a LAN environment according to the following menu selections in the Options menu of Virus Clinic. It is assumed that if a virus is detected, the user will notify you to assist with the virus removal.

Clinic	Setting
Allow Repair	off
Allow Delete	off
Allow Reinoc	off
Allow Cancel	off
Allow Repair All	off
Allow Delete All	off
Allow Reinoc All	off
Allow Scanning of Network Drives	off

Intercept	Setting
Enable Beep Alert	Yes
Enable Popup Alert	Yes
Seconds to display Popup Alert Box	30
Enable Log to File	Yes
FileName:	F:\AUDIT.LOG
Allow Proceed	off
Allow Reinoculate	off

Global	Setting
Detect Unknown Viruses	Yes
Auto-inoculate	Yes
Scan Executables Only	Yes
Network Inoculation Directory	\NCDTREE
Virus Alert Custom Message	Please Call The LAN Admin. at 1234
Password	Be sure to set the password so only you can change the configuration.

Version 2.5 Network Improvements

Norton AntiVirus Version 2.5 adds several network enhancements. Norton AntiVirus can be configured to automatically send a broadcast to a central node whenever a virus is detected. This instantly alerts the LAN administrator of any virus activity on the LAN. Note that this feature is only available on Novell Netware LANs.

Summary

Yes, viruses can spread like wildfire on a LAN, but a properly configured LAN can halt the virus spread and is safer than sneaker net.

Boot-sector viruses, by nature, don't spread on a LAN, but program-infecting viruses spread very quickly. Using the network's built-in security features and running Norton AntiVirus on the workstations will keep viruses from your LAN.

Fighting viruses on a LAN demands that you know the LAN well and that you painstakingly track down every occurrence of the virus infection.

Technically speaking, there is a way to transmit a boot sector over a modem. Teledisk, a shareware program, can take an entire diskette, including the boot sector, and compress it into one file. The receiving end uses Teledisk to put the file back onto a diskette. This process is not common and cannot happen by accident. Virus researchers use Teledisk to submit virus samples of boot sector viruses.

The Norton
AntiVirus Files

File	Purpose
CLEANUP.DOC	Documentation for CLEANUP.EXE
CLEANUP.EXE	Removes Norton AntiVirus version 1.5 inoculation files
INSTALL.CFG	INSTALL.EXE Configuration
INSTALL.EXE	Norton AntiVirus Install Program
NAV&.SYS	Virus Intercept-Execution Only Scan—loads as a device driver in CONFIG.SYS
NAV.EXE	Virus Clinic for DOS
NAV.HLP	Virus Clinic Help System
NAV.ICO	Virus Intercept (NAVPOPUP.EXE) Icon for Windows
NAV_.SYS	Virus Intercept Comprehensive scan
NAVDLL.DLL	Windows Norton AntiVirus Support File
NAVDOS5.HLP	Added to DOS 5 Help system during installation
NAVPOPUP.EXE	Virus Intercept—Windows popup alert
NAVPOPUP.HLP	Help for Virus Intercept—Windows popup alert
NAVSETUP.EXE	Configures Startup, Video, and Mouse options without running Virus Clinic
NAVUTIL.DLL	Support File for NAVW.EXE in Windows
NAVW.EXE	Windows Virus Clinic
NAVW.GRP	Windows Group file
NAVW.HL	Help for Windows Virus Clinic
NSETUP.CFG	Configuration information for NAVSETUP.EXE
NSETUP.OVL	Overlay for NAVSETUP.EXE
READ.ME	Last minute release information concerning Norton AntiVirus. READ.ME provides information not in the documentation.
RESCUE.EXE	Creates and restores system information
VNAVD.386	Windows Virtual Device Driver

Virus Information

This virus information is listed in the following categories:

Viruses by Infection Spread

Viruses by Virus Type

Viruses by Origin

Viruses by Activation Date

Virus Descriptions

Viruses by Infection Spread

Common

903	Evil Empire
1381	Evil Empire-B
1554	Fellowship
1575	Flip
4096	FORM-Virus
5120	Haifa
AirCop	Invader
Alameda	Invol
Anarkia	Jerusalem
Anti-Tel	Joshi
Azusa	Keypress
Bloody!	Lehigh
Brain	Liberty
Cascade	Loa Duong
Cascade-B	Maltese Amoeba
Dark Avenger	Michelangelo
DataLock	Microbes
Den Zuk	MusicBug
Dir-2	NoInt
Disk Killer	Nomenklatura
Dutch 555	Ohio
EDV	Ontario

Perfume	SVC 5.0
Ping Pong-B	SVC 6.0
Plastique	Taiwan 3
Possessed	Taiwan 4
Print Screen	Telecom
R-11	Tequila
Slayer Family	V2000
Slow	V2100
StarDot 600	Vacsina
Stoned	Vienna
Striker #1	Violator
Sunday	Yankee Doodle

Viruses by Virus Type

Boot-Sector Viruses

AirCop	EDV
Alameda	Evil Empire
Anti-Tel	Evil Empire-B
Ashar	Filler
Azusa	FORM-Virus
Bloody!	Guillon
Brain	Horse Boot
Cannabis	Joshi
Catman	Keydrop
Chaos	Korea
Den Zuk	Loa Duong
Disk Killer	Mardi Bros

Michelangelo	Ping Pong-B
Microbes	Print Screen
MusicBug	Stoned
NoInt	Swap
Ohio	Swedish Disaster
Pentagon	Tony Boot
Ping Pong	Windmill

Stealth and Sub-Stealth Viruses

512	Holocaust
1008	Joshi
1024 SBC	Leech
1963	Lucifer
2560	Magnitogorsk 2048
4096	MG
Ah	MG-2
Anti-Tel	Murphy
Brain	Naughty Hacker Family
Brothers	NoInt
Casino	PCV
Caz	Plovdiv 1.1
Damage	Plovdiv 1.3
Dir-2	Pregnant
EDV	R-11
Filler	Sentinel
Finnish-709	Sunday-2
Fish	SVC 4.0
Gremlin	SVC 5.0

SVC 6.0

Telecom

Tequila

Twin-351

V651

V1024

V2000

V2100

Whale

Windmill

Zero Bug

ZeroHunt

Viruses by Origin

Argentina

Ada

Error

Australia

Australian

Australian 403

Growing Block

Liberty

Possessed

Slow

Viper

Austria

1253

Vienna

Belgium

Got-You

Bolivia

Miky

Bulgaria

512

1226

1226D

Anthrax

Anti-Pascal

Anti-Pascal II

Boys

Brainy

Dark Avenger

Dark Lord

Darth Vader

Destructor V4.00

Dir-2

ETC

Evil

Happy New Year

Horse Boot

Kamikazi

Leech

MG

MG-2

Mini-45

Multi-123

Murphy

Mutant Family

Naughty Hacker Family

Nina

Parity

Phoenix

Phoenix 2000

PhoenixD

Proud

Sentinel

Shake

Tiny Family

Tony

Tony Boot

V82

V651

V800

V1024

V2000

V2100

Vacsina

VFSI

VHP

VHP2

Warrior

Yankee Doodle

Yankee 2

Canada

1024 SBC

Amilia

Arf

Evil Empire

Evil Empire-B

Holland Girl 2

NoInt

Ontario

Ontario 730

R-10

R-11

Rage

Sicilian Mob

Small-38

Sunday-2

Violator

Violator B4

Yukon Overwriting

Commonwealth States

2560

Akuku

Attention!

Bebe	USSR 600
Best Wishes	USSR 707
Catman	USSR 711
Crash	USSR 948
Dir Virus	USSR 1049
F-Word	USSR 2144
Hymn	Victor
Kemerovo	Voronezh
Kiev 483	WordSwap
Label	*Czechoslovakia*
Lozinsky	Blinker
Magnitogorsk 2048	Semtex
MGTU	Shaker
NTKC	*Denmark*
Red Diavolyata	Kennedy
SVC 3.1	Tiny Virus
SVC 4.0	*England*
SVC 5.0	Chaos
SVC 6.0	Typo COM
Sverdlov	VP
Tumen V.5	*Finland*
Tumen V2.0	1008
USSR	Cinderella
USSR 311	Crew-2480
USSR 492	Finnish-709
USSR 516	Relzfu

France

903

EDV

Mardi Bros

Paris

Germany

405

5120

Ambulance Car

Burger

Cascade

Cascade-B

CD

Christmas Tree

Eight Tunes

Fingers

Fish

Flash

Halloechen

Kalah

Karin

Number One

Perfume

RaubKopie

RPVS

VCS

VirDem

Whale

Greece

Armagedon

Pixel

Hong Kong

Azusa

Hungary

Filler

Monxla

Monxla B

Phantom

Polimer

Turbo 448

Turbo Kukac

Iceland

Ghostballs

Icelandic

Icelandic-II

Icelandic-III

India

Joshi

Microbes

Print Screen

Indonesia

1392

Den Zuk

Ohio

Ireland

    Suriv 4.02

Israel

    4096

    Alabama

    Do-Nothing

    Haifa

    JoJo

    Mix1

    Saddam

    Suriv 1.01

    Suriv 2.01

    Suriv 3.00

    Swap

    Typo Boot

Italy

    Ah

    AntiChrist

    Bandit

    Cracker Jack

    Damage

    Enigma

    Erasmus

    Goblin

    Hero

    HIV

    I-B

    Interceptor

    Italian 803

    Italian Pest

    Itavir

    Jerusalem

    Kamasya

    Klaeren

    Little Pieces

    Lucifer

    Migram

    PCV

    Smack

    Xabaras

Korea

    Korea

Malaysia

    Black Monday

    Fellowship

Malta

    Casino

    Maltese Amoeba

Mexico

    Devil's Dance

Netherlands

    Cannabis

    Datacrime

    Datacrime-B

Datacrime II

Datacrime IIB

Deicide

Dutch 555

Dutch Tiny

Gotcha

Grapje

Groen Links

Holland Girl

Little Brother

Mini-97

New Jerusalem

Nomenklatura

Payday

Zero Bug

New Zealand

Jerusalem 1776

Shadow

Stoned

Pakistan

Brain

Philippines

Revenge Attacker

Windmill

Poland

Dot Killer

Father Christmas

Gosia

Hybryd

Joker

Mono

MPS 1.1

MPS 3.1

MPS 3.2

Polish 217

Polish 529

Polish 583

Polish-45

Polish-376

Self

Stone '90

SVir

VComm

W13

Portugal

Amstrad

Lisbon

Pirate

Republic of South Africa

African 109

Blood

Friday the 13th COM

June 16th

Pathhunt

Poem

Saturday the 14th

StinkFoot

Saudi Arabia

834

Spain

1210

1720

Anti-Tel

Barcelona

Cara

Caz

Holocaust

July 13th

Spanish

Spanish April Fools

Telecom

Sweden

Swedish Disaster

Tormentor

Tormentor-1072

Switzerland

Burghofer

Flip

FORM-Virus

Swiss 143

Tequila

Taiwan

382 Recovery

1575

Bloody!

Disk Killer

Doom II

Invader

MusicBug

Plastique

Plastique-B

Spyer

Taiwan

Taiwan 3

Taiwan 4

Wolfman

Thailand

Loa Duong

Mule

United States

1260

AirCop

Alameda

DataLock

dBASE

Doom II-B

Frere Jacques

Frog's Alley

Green Peace

Grither

Guppy

Hastings

Invol

Iraqui Warrior

Jeff

JoJo 2

Keypress

Lehigh

Leprosy

Leprosy-3

Patient

Pixie

Psychogenius

Saratoga

Scott's Valley

Solano 2000

Striker #1

Subliminal 1.10

Sunday

Tester

The Plague

Timid

Traveller

V2P2

V2P6

V2P6Z

V801

Virus-90

Virus-101

Westwood

Wisconsin

Yap

ZeroHunt

ZK900

Viruses by Activation Date

Activation Date/Day of Week	Virus Name
Sundays (any)	Sunday
	Sunday-2
Mondays (any)	Garfield
	I-B (BadGuy)
	I-B (BadGuy 2)
	I-B (Exterminator)
Tuesdays (any)	Ah
	I-B (Demon)
	I-B (Demon-B)
	Kamasya
Tuesday the 13ths	Jerusalem (Anarkia)
Wednesdays (any)	Victor
Thursday the 12ths	CD
Fridays (any)	Frere Jacques
	Smack
Friday not the 13ths	Jerusalem (Payday)
Friday the 13ths	1720
	Friday the 13th COM
	Jerusalem
	RAM Virus
	Suriv 3.00
	Westwood
Friday the 13ths (starting in 1992)	Hybryd
Fridays after 15th of Month	Jerusalem (Skism-1)

continues

Activation Date/Day of Week	Virus Name
Saturdays (any)	Italian Pest (Finger)
	Jerusalem (Phenome)
	Migram
Saturday the 14ths	Saturday the 14th
2nd day of any month	Flip
5th day of any month	Frog's Alley
8th day of any month	Taiwan
10th day of any month	Day10
13th day of any month	Monxla
18th day of any month	FORM-Virus (Form-18)
20th day of any month	Day10
24th day of any month	FORM-Virus
30th day of any month	Day10
January 1st-September 21st	Plastique (COBOL)
January 5th	Joshi
January 15th	Casino
January 25th	Jerusalem (January 25th)
February 2nd	Amilia
March (any day)	903
March 6th	Michelangelo
March 15th	Maltese Amoeba
April 1st	Casper
	Christmas Tree
	Suriv 1.01
	Suriv 2.01
	Suriv 4.02
April 15th	Casino
	Murphy (Swami)

Activation Date/Day of Week	Virus Name
May 1st thru May 4th	1210
June 6th	Kennedy
June 16th	June 16th
July-December	Got-You
	Jerusalem (Jerusalem-PLO)
	Jerusalem (Mendoza)
July 13th	July 13th
August 15th	Casino
August 16th	August 16th
September 1st-September 30th	1554
	1704 Format
	AirCop (AirCop-B)
	Cascade
	Cascade-B
September 4th	Violator (Violator B1)
September 20th-December 31st	Plastique
	Plastique-B
September 22nd-December 31st	4096
October 1st-December 31st	1554
	1704 Format
	4096
	Cascade
	Cascade-B
October 4th	Violator (Violator B1)
October 12th	Jerusalem (Anarkia-B)
October 13th-December 31st	Datacrime
	Datacrime-B

continues

Activation Date/Day of Week	Virus Name
	Datacrime II
	Datacrime IIB
October 23rd	Karin
October 31st	Halloween
	Violator (Violator B2)
November 1st	Maltese Amoeba
November 4th	Violator (Violator B1)
November 17th	November 17th
November 18th	Kennedy
November 22nd	Kennedy
November 30th	Jerusalem 11-30
December 1st-December 31st	1253
December 4th	Violator (Violator B1)
December 19th-December 31st	Father Christmas
December 21st	Poem
December 24th	Icelandic-III
December 24th-January 1st	Christmas Tree
December 25th	Christmas In Japan
	Violator (Violator B3)
December 28th	Spanish April Fools
December 31st	Violator (Violator B2)
After August 1, 1989	Fu Manchu
After June, 1990	Flash
After August, 1990	DataLock
After August 14, 1990	Violator
After November 11, 1990	Fingers
After December 31, 1991	Sicilian Mob
Year is 1992	Europe-92
	Year 1992

Virus Index

Information on known viruses, including test results of Norton AntiVirus's effectivness against them. (Based on NAV 2.0 list of Viruses.)

Total definitions: 347

Total strains: 1,012

Virus Information Souce: Peter Norton Technical Support, Patricia Hoffman's Virus Information Summary List, In-Lab Testing

12 Tricks Trojan

> Spread: Common (Europe and Canada)
>
> Infects: Trojan Horse program infects Master Boot Record
>
> Length: n/a
>
> Symptoms: Randomly performs one of the following twelve tricks:

1. Random delay loop in the timer tick—PC runs slow and jerky.

2. End of Interrupt inserted to Timer Tick—diskette drive runs, clock stops, some TSRs affected.

3. Timer tick altered with every keystroke—TIME results in divide overflow, programs may crash.

4. 25% of Interrupt 0dh (printer) nulled.

5. 25% of Interrupt 0eh (floppy) nulled.

6. Random delay loop added to interrupt 10h (video)—PC runs slow and video display is very jerky.

7. Video scroll altered to video blank.

8. All diskette drives altered to diskette write requests.

9. Caps Lock, Num Lock, and Shift are randomly altered with every keystroke.

10. All printing is completely garbled.

11. Printing cases are reversed, line feeds canceled, spaces canceled.

12. Clock not updated, cannot be changed.

144

Alias: AT144

Spread: Rare

Infects: .COM, COMMAND.COM on AT, 386, and 486 PCs

Length: 144

Symptoms: File date/time changes, XT class PC hang.

217

Aliases: Polish Stupid, Polish 217, V217

Spread: Rare

Infects: one .COM program file in current directory each time infected program is executed, can infect COMMAND.COM

Length: 217

Symptoms: If COMMAND.COM is infected, system will reboot.

382 (2)

Aliases: 382 Recovery, Recovery

Spread: Rare

Infects: .COM

Length: first 382 bytes overwritten

Symptoms: Boot failures, diskette drives spin out of control, system hangs, strange random characters appear on the screen.

405 (3)

Aliases: Hammelburg, 405-EST

Spread: Extinct

Infects: .COM files in the Root

Length: overwrites first

Symptoms:

453 RPVS (2)

> Aliases: 453, RPVS, TUQ
>
> Spread: Endangered
>
> Infects: one .COM program file each time the virus is executed
>
> Length: 453
>
> Internal Message: TUQ.RPVS (a series of PUSH instructions)
>
> Symptoms: No activation logic, only replication.

492 (2)

> Aliases: USSR 492, RC492
>
> Spread: Rare
>
> Infects: .COM
>
> Length: 492
>
> Symptoms: File date/time changed to date/time of infection.

512 (7)

> Aliases: Number of the Beast, Stealth Virus
>
> Spread: Rare
>
> Infects: .COM
>
> Length: 512
>
> Internal Message: 666
>
> Symptoms: Program crashes, system hangs, running CHKDSK may cause file allocation damage.

512-E

> Spread: Rare
>
> Infects: .COM, will load TSR in video memory
>
> Length: 512
>
> Symptoms: Variant of 512, program crashes, system hangs, running CHKDSK may cause file allocation damage.

529 (2)

> Aliases: Polish 529, Piter2
>
> Spread: Rare
>
> Infects: .COM
>
> Length: 529
>
> Symptoms: Virus replication only.

691

> Aliases: Dir Virus
>
> Spread: Rare
>
> Infects: .COM program files during DIR commands
>
> Length: 691
>
> Symptoms: Slow execution of DIR commands, running CHKDSK may cause file allocation errors.

777 Virus

> Alias: Revenge Attacker
>
> Spread: Rare
>
> Infects: .COM, COMMAND.COM
>
> Length: 777
>
> Internal Messages: "*** 777 - Revenge Attacker V1.01 *** ," "*.COM"
>
> Symptoms: Erroneous DIR command results, activates when all .COM programs in the current directory have been infected; 777 then overwrites the hard disk.

855

> Alias: November 17th
>
> Spread: New
>
> Infects: .COM, .EXE
>
> Length: 855
>
> Internal Message: SCAN.CLEAN.COMEXE
>
> Symptoms: Replication only.

900

Aliases: Pray, ZK900

Spread: Rare

Infects: .COM, .EXE

Length: 900

Internal Message: infected programs end with: "zx"

Symptoms: Plays the tune "Pray for the dead, and the dead will pray for you" every 3-5 minutes.

903

Aliases: FichV, CHV 2.1

Stealth: Accelerated Infector

Spread: Common

Infects: .COM, COMMAND.COM

Length: 903

Message: When COMMAND.COM is infected the message Fichier introuvable may be displayed

Symptoms: Possible system hangs. During March the first six sectors of each track of the current hard disk will be overwritten with the French phrase "CHV 2.1 vous a eu" (English: "CHV 2.1 got you").

1008

Aliases: Suomi, Oulu

Spread: Rare

Infects: COMMAND.COM

Length: 1008

Symptoms: COMMAND.COM file growth by 1008. File Growth is hidden if virus is live in memory. Possible Stack error when booting an infected PC.

1024PSCR (Print Screen)

Spread: Rare

Infects: .COM

Length: 1024

Symptoms: Pressing Print Screen will display the CMOS instead of printing the screen.

1049

Aliases: USSR 1049, RCE-1049

Spread: Rare

Infects: .COM, .EXE

Length: 1049

Symptoms: Sometimes this virus will cause the PC to hang when infecting .EXE files. Otherwise, the 1049 only replicates.

1067

Spread: Rare

Infects: .COM, COMMAND.COM

Length: 1067

Symptoms: Executing infected .EXE file may cause an error message: Program too big to fit in memory.

1075

Aliases: Crash, Russ-1075, DBF Blank

Spread: Rumored

Infects: fails to replicate

Length: 1075

Symptoms: Sample viruses crash and do not load into memory or infect other files.

1168 (4)

Aliases: DataCrime, Columbus Day

Spread: Extinct

Infects: .COM

Length: 1168

Message: `DATACRIME VIRUS`

`RELEASED: 1 MARCH 1989`

Symptoms: Lowlevel format of MFM hard disks.

1210 (5)

Alias: Prudents

Spread: Rare

Infects: .EXE

Length: 1210

Symptoms: May 1st to May 4th disk writes are altered to disk verifies causing a disk write failure.

1280 (3)

Aliases: Datacrime-B, Columbus Day

Spread: Extinct

Infects: .EXE

Length: 1280

Symptoms: Formats MFM/RLL hard disks, diskette drive access unreliable.

1381 (2)

Alias: Internal

Spread: Common

Infects: one .EXE program file each time the virus is executed

Length: 1381 - 1395

Message: INTERNAL ERROR 02CH

PLEASE CONTACT YOUR HARDWARE MANUFACTURER IMMEDIATELY !

DO NOT FORGET TO REPORT THE ERROR CODE !

Symptoms: The message is displayed and the currently running program is disinfected.

1554

Aliases: Ten Bytes, 9800:0000 Virus, V-Alert, 1559 5

Spread: Rare

Infects: .COM, .EXE

Length: 1554 - 1569

Symptoms: Sept., Oct., Nov. or Dec.: Program and Data files corrupted. All files written to the disk will be missing the first ten bytes; the last ten bytes will be random characters.

1591

Aliases: Green Caterpillar, 1575, 1577

Spread: Common

Infects: One .COM, .EXE program file with every DIR or COPY command. Immediately infects COMMAND.COM.

Length: 1577 - 1591

Symptoms: File date and time will be changed to the date and time of the infection. Some 1591 strains display a green caterpillar at the bottom of the screen similar to the Centipede arcade game.

1605 (2)

Aliases: 1605-B, 1600, Antiscan, Tel Aviv, Solomon Virus

Spread: Rare

Infects: .COM, .EXE (not COMMAND.COM)

Length: .COM: 1605, .EXE: 1601 - 1610

Symptoms: 15-20% system slowdown.

170X (32)

> Alias: 1704 Format
>
> Spread: Rare
>
> Infects: .COM
>
> Length: 1704
>
> Symptoms: During Oct., Nov., Dec. formats the hard disk.

1720 (5)

> Alias: PSQR Virus (Jerusalem Variant)
>
> Spread: Rare
>
> Infects: .COM, .EXE
>
> Length: .COM: 1720, .EXE: 1719 - 1733
>
> Message: infected programs contain string: "PSQR"
>
> Symptoms: On any Friday 13th, this virus will delete any program executed and will destroy the hard disk's boot sector and partition table.

1961 (4)

> Aliases: Yankee 2, Yankee Virus, Yankee-go-Home, Old Yankee
>
> Spread: Endangered
>
> Infects: .EXE
>
> Length: 1961 - 1624
>
> Symptoms: Plays Yankee Doodle whenever it finds a new .EXE file to infect.

1963

> Aliases: V1963, 1963 OverWrite (related to Dark Avenger)
>
> Stealth: Disinfector
>
> Spread: Rare
>
> Infects: .COM, .EXE, COMMAND.COM

Length: 1963

Symptoms: Running CHKDSK may cause file allocation errors.

2144 (2)

Aliases: USSR 2144, V2144, USSR 2144-B

Spread: Rare

Infects: .COM, .EXE

Length: 2144

Symptoms: Replication only.

2559 Virus

Aliases: 2623, Yaunch

Spread: Rare

Infects: .EXE

Length: 2559 - 2933

Symptoms: Possible system hangs and unexpected disk/diskette access.

2930/3066 (19)

Aliases: TraceBack, TraceBack II, 3066

Spread: Extinct

Infects: .COM, .EXE

Length: 2930

Symptoms: At one-hour intervals, the characters will fall to the bottom of the screen. After one minute they return to the original position and the PC can continue operation.

3551 (10)

Aliases: Syslock, 3555, Macho-A, Advent, Advent-B

Spread: Endangered

Infects: .COM and .EXE program files

Length: 3551

Symptoms: Replace "Microsoft" with "MACROSOFT." Advent variants will play "Oh Tannenbaum" (Oh Christmas Tree) during December.

4096 (6)

Aliases: Frodo, Century Virus, Stealth Virus, 100 Years Virus

Stealth: Accelerated Infector, Dissimulator

Spread: Common

Infects: .COM, .EXE, .OVL

Length: 4096

Internal Message: FRODO LIVES

Symptoms: Very slowly cross-links files, hangs on Sept. 22 (Frodo Baggins' Birthday).

5120 (6)

Aliases: VBASIC Virus, Basic Virus

Spread: Common

Infects: .COM, .EXE, COMMAND.COM

Length: 5120

Internal Message:

BASRUN

BRUN

IBMBIO.COM

IBMDOS.COM

COMMAND.COM

Access denied

Symptoms: Possible file corruption and unexpected disk activity.

7808

Spread: Rare

Infects: .COM, .EXE

Length: 7808

Symptoms: Date/time changes, "not enough memory" errors.

A-403 (2)

Aliases: 403, Australian 403, Zeroto-O

Spread: Rare

Infects: .COM, COMMAND.COM

Length: 403

Symptoms: File date/time changes to date/time of infection, infected programs may not execute properly.

Adolph Trojan

Alias: V2P6

Spread: Rare

Infects: .COM

Length: 2109 - 2445

Symptoms: Replication.

AIDS (3)

Aliases: Hahaha, Taunt, VGA2CGA, Burger.Pascal

Spread: Endangered

Infects: .COM

Length: Overwriting—no file growth

Symptoms: .COM file corruption. When the virus activates, it displays the message Your computer now has AIDS.

Aids-2

Alias: Companion Virus

Stealth: Multipartite Infector

Spread: Endangered

Infects: Creates infected .COM version of .EXE program files

Length: 8064

Symptoms: After creating infected .COM file, Aids-2 plays a melody and displays:

```
Your computer is infected with ...
♥ "Symbol" AIDS Virus II ♥
- Signed WOP & PGT of DutchCrack -
Getting used to me?
Next time, use a Condom .....
```

Aircop (2)

Spread: Common

Infects: Boot sector

Length: Memory decrease of 1024

Symptoms: Randomly displays: `Red State, Germ Offensive. AIRCOP`. Also may cause Stack Overflow errors and system halts. AirCop-B displays `This is Aircop`.

Akuku

Alias: Metal Thunder

Stealth: Accelerated Infector

Spread: Rare

Infects: Three .COM and .EXE program files (including COMMAND.COM) each time the virus is executed

Length: 891

Hidden Message: "A kuku, Nastepny komornik !!!," or "(c) by Metal Thunder IVRL MI."

Symptoms: Executing .EXE files may result in `Error in EXE file` message. Also, there may be unexpected hard disk access.

Alabama (7)

Spread: Endangered

Infects: .EXE

Length: 1560

Symptoms: Displays the following message at one-hour intervals:

```
SOFTWARE COPIES PROHIBITED BY INTERNATIONAL LAW
Box 1055 Tuscambia ALABAMA USA.
```

On Fridays, this virus will swap FAT entries, slowly corrupting files.

Ambulance

Aliases: Ambulance Car, RedX, Red Cross

Spread: Rare

Infects: one .COM program file every time the virus is executed (but not COMMAND.COM)

Length: 796

Symptoms: On a random basis (about 1%), a character-block graphic display of an ambulance will move left to right across the bottom of the screen with a siren sound.

Amoeba (2)

Alias: 1392

Spread: Rare

Infects: .COM, .EXE

Length: 1392

Internal Message: "SMA KHETAPUNK - Nouvel Band A.M.O.E.B.A"

Symptoms: File date changed to date of infection.

Amstrad (4)

> Spread: Endangered
>
> Infects: .COM, COMMAND.COM
>
> Length: 847
>
> Symptoms: (Based on Pixel Virus) Possible system hangs. Program is overwritten and it displays the message:
>
> ```
> =!= Buy AMSTRAD it is THE CHEAPEST COMPUTER that you
> can buy
> ```
>
> the Amstrad-End Is Near variant displays:
>
> ```
> =!= THE END IS NEAR!!
>
>  THE SIGNS OF THE BEAST ARE EVERYWHERE
> ```
>
> the Amstrad-Luz displays:
>
> ```
> =!= Hello, John Mcafee,please upgrade me.
>
> Best regards, Jean Luz.
> ```

ANSI Trojan

> Spread: Common
>
> Infects: ANSI text files
>
> Symptoms: Remaps keyboard to cause destructive effects.

Anthrax (3)

> Spread: Rare
>
> Infects: .COM, .EXE, Partition Table
>
> Length: 1040 - 1279
>
> Internal Message: (c) Damage, Inc. ANTHRAX Sophia 1990
>
> Symptoms: Replicates.

Anti-Pascal (4)

> Aliases: Anti-Pascal 605 Virus, AP-605, C-605, V605
>
> Spread: Rare (Escaped Research)
>
> Infects: .COM

Length: 605

Symptoms: Corrupts .BAK and .PAS files.

Anti-Pascal-2 (2)

Aliases: Anti-Pascal 400, AP-400

Spread: Research

Infects: .COM

Length: 400

Symptoms: Corrupts .BAK, .BAT and .PAS files. Boot sector alteration.

Anticad (2)

Aliases: 1253, V-1, Thanksgiving

Spread: Rare

Infects: .COM, some variants of COMMAND.COM

Length: 1253

Symptoms: Partition table changes, infected program will have the 4th through 6th byte changed to V-1. On December 24th it will overwrite the current drive (diskette or hard drive).

Armageddon (2)

Aliases: Armagedon The First, Armagedon The Greek, Armagedon-1077

Spread: Rare

Infects: .COM

Length: 1079

Symptoms: Message Armagedon the GREEK sent to a COM port at timed intervals, also attempts to call Local Time Information in Crete, Greece.

Azusa

Alias: Hong Kong

Spread: Very Common

Infects: Boot sector and partition table

Length: available system memory 1024 or 2048 bytes less

Symptoms: LTP1 and COM ports may be disabled, diskettes may be corrupted.

Bad Boy-1

Spread: Rare

Infects: .COM, COMMAND.COM

Length: 1,000

Hidden Message:

"The bad boy halt your system ..."

"The Bad Boy virus, Copyright (C) 1991."

Symptoms: Random activation results in scrolling characters, then system hangs.

Bad Boy-2

Spread: Rare

Infects: .COM, COMMAND.COM

Length: 1,000

Hidden Message:

"Make me better!"

"The Bad Boy virus, Version 2.0, Copyright (C) 1991."

Symptoms: Activates less frequently than Bad Boy 1, but with the same results.

Bandit

Spread: Research (based on Enigma virus)

Infects: .EXE

Length: 1641

Internal Message:

"*.* *.exe wwZZZZ"

"!!PCBANDIT!!"

Symptoms: Replication only.

Best Wishes

Spread: Rare

Infects: .COM, COMMAND.COM

Length: 970

Symptoms: Boot sector modification, file/date changes, possible system hangs.

Bljec (7)

Aliases: family of viruses: Bljec3, Bljec3B, Bljec4, Bljec5, Bljec5B, Bljec6, Bljec7, Bljec7B, Bljec8, Bljec9, Bljec9B

Spread: Rare

Infects: .COM

Length: 231 - 374

Symptoms: System hangs, file/date changes, Write Fault errors on device PRN, possible Boot Failures.

Blood

Alias: Blood2

Spread: Rare

Infects: .COM program files

Length: 418

Symptoms: Cursor cascade effect, random characters and, after August 15th, system reboots or hangs.

Bloody! (2)

Aliases: Beijing, June 4th

Spread: Common

Infects: Boot sector and partition table

Length: system memory decrease of 2048 bytes

Symptoms: 128th boot and every sixth boot thereafter displays the message Bloody! Jun. 4, 1989 (the date of the confrontation in Beijing, China between Chinese students and the Chinese Army).

Bloomington

> Aliases: NoInt, LastDirSect, Stoned III
>
> Stealth: Dissimulator variant of Stoned virus
>
> Spread: Common
>
> Infects: Boot sector and partition table
>
> Length: memory decrease of 2048
>
> Symptoms: Diskette directory corruption.

Boys Virus

> Spread: Rare
>
> Infects: .COM
>
> Length: 500
>
> Internal Message:
>
> "The good and the bad boy."
>
> "*.EXE"
>
> "????????COM"
>
> Symptoms: Sets the System attribute of .EXE files making those files hidden, and then attempts to copy the (apparently missing) files back on to the disk results in File Creation Error message because the .EXE file is still there.

Brain-A/B (8)

> Aliases: Pakistani, Pakistani Brain, Clone, Nipper
>
> Stealth: Dissimulator
>
> Spread: Common
>
> Infects: Boot sector
>
> Length: 3096 - 7500
>
> Symptoms: Extended Boot time, Volume Label changed to "(c) Brain."

Burger (4)

Aliases: family of viruses: 404, 505, 509, 537, 540, 541, 560, 560-B, 909090h, CIA

Spread: Rare

Infects: .COM, .EXE

Length: 560

Symptoms: Infected programs are overwritten and will not run.

Burger-B

Alias: 560-B

Spread: Rare

Infects: .COM, .EXE

Length: 560

Internal message: "his program downloaded from the Vir"

Symptoms: Infected program will not run.

Carioca

Spread: Rare

Infects: .COM

Length: 951

Symptoms: Replication only.

Cascade-170X (4)

Aliases: Blackjack, Fall, Falling Letters, 1701, 1704, 1701 Mutation, 1704-B, Cunning, 1704-Format

Spread: Common

Infects: .COM

Length: 1701 or 1704

Symptoms: During the months of fall (Oct., Nov. and Dec.) the letters will randomly fall from the screen. Cunning variant plays music. Cascade 1704-Format variant formats the hard disk.

Casino

> Spread: Rare
>
> Infects: .COM
>
> Length: 2330
>
> Symptoms: File allocation errors, slot machine game, and partition table damage.

Catman

> Spread: Rare
>
> Infects: Boot sector and partition table via dropper program
>
> Length:
>
> Symptoms: Booting with an infected partition table may result in system hang.

Christmas (2)

> Aliases: Christmas Tree, Tannenbaum, XA1, 1539
>
> Stealth: Polymorphic Infector
>
> Spread: Endangered
>
> Infects: .COM
>
> Length: 1539
>
> Symptoms: On April 1, destroys the partition table, also from Dec. 24 to Jan. 1 displays full-screen picture of Christmas tree.

Christmas in Japan

> Aliases: Japanese Christmas, Xmas in Japan
>
> Spread: Rare
>
> Infects: .COM
>
> Length: 600
>
> Symptoms: On December 25th, displays A merry Christmas to you.

Cinderella

Spread: Rare

Infects: .COM

Length: 390

Hidden Message: cInDeReL.la

Symptoms: Replication only.

Crew-2480

Aliases: 2480, V2480

Spread: Rare

Infects: .COM from January through May

Length: 2480

Symptoms: File date/time change, system hangs, may display message `European Cracking Crew`.

CVIR

Alias: Nowhere Man, CVirus

Spread: Rare

Infects: .COM, .EXE

Length: 6286

Symptoms: Program truncated, long program load then program won't execute, also once all files are infected the virus will display the message `All files infected. Mission complete.`

Damage-B

Spread: Rare

Infects: .COM, .EXE, COMMAND.COM

Length: 1063

Internal message: "DAMAGE!!!!" or "Jump for Joy!!! DAMAGE-B"

Symptoms: At a few second before 3 p.m. a large multicolored diamond appears on-screen and breaks into smaller diamonds that shoot around the screen and destroy characters.

Dark Avenger (4)

Aliases: Black Avenger, Boroda, Eddie, Diana, Rabid Avenger, VAN Soft, Dark Avenger 1801, Dark Avenger-C, Dark Avenger-D, PS!KO, Evil Men

Spread: Very Common

Infects: .COM, .EXE, .SYS program files

Length: 1800

Internal Message:

Eddie Lives...somewhere in time!

Diana P.

This program was written in the city of Sofia

(c)1988-1989 Dark Avenger

Symptoms: File/disk corruption (variants each have a different message).

Data Crime II (8)

Aliases: 1514, Columbus Day

Stealth: Multipartite Infector

Spread: Endangered

Infects: .COM, .EXE files on MFM drives

Length: 1514

Symptoms: Formats disk except on Mondays.

Data Crime II-B (4)

Spread: Endangered

Infects: .COM, .EXE

Length: 1917

Symptoms: Formats disks (except on Mondays), floppy disk access.

DataLock (2)

    Aliases: DataLock 1.00, V920

    Spread: Common

    Infects: .EXE, COMMAND.COM

    Length: 920

    Symptoms: File date/time changed to date/time of infection, `out of file handle` errors.

DataRape v2.0

    Aliases: R-10, DataRape-10, Rape-10

    Spread: Rare

    Infects: .COM

    Length: 500

    Symptoms: Randomly activates then overwrites and formats the hard disk.

DBase

    Alias: DBF Virus

    Spread: Extinct

    Infects: .COM, .OVL

    Length: 1864

    Symptoms: Hides corruption of .dbf files—removal of virus will result in corrupted .DBF file, after 90 days FAT and root directory are overwritten.

Dear Nina

    Aliases: Happy New Year, Happy N.Y., V1600

    Spread: Rare

    Infects: .COM, .EXE

    Length: 1600

Internal Message:

"Dear Nina, you make me write this virus; Happy new year!"

"1989"

Symptoms: Diskette boot sector altered, boot failures, bad or missing command interpreter.

Deicide (2)

Alias: Glen

Spread: Rare

Infects: .COM

Length: 666

Internal message:

"This experimental virus was written by Glenn Benton

to see if I can make a virus while learning machinecode

for 2,5 months. (C) 10-23-1990 by Glenn.

I keep on going making viruses."

Symptoms: FAT Corruption and system hangs. If the virus does not find .COM to infect, the following message appears:

```
DEICIDE!

Glenn (666) says : BYE BYE HARDDISK!!

Next time be carufull with illegal stuff
```

and then the virus overwrites the first 80 sectors of the hard disk.

Den Zuk (3)

Aliases: Search, Venezuelan

Spread: Common

Infects: Diskette Boot sector

Length:

Internal Message:

"Welcome to the

C l u b

—The HackerS—

Hackin'

All The Time

The HackerS"

Symptoms: Booting with an infected diskette displays a purple message, DEN ZUK, and the diskette label changes to "Y.C.1.E.R.P." if the diskette was previously infected with Brain.

Destructor (2)

Alias: Destructor V4.00

Spread: Rare

Infects: .COM, .EXE

Length: 1150 - 1162

Internal message: "DESTRUCTOR V4.00 (c) 1990 by ATA"

Symptoms: Replication only.

Devil's Dance (8)

Mexican, Devil's Dance-B, Batman, Dance

Spread: Rare

Infects: .COM

Length: 941

Symptoms: A warm boot will result in the following message:

Have you ever danced with the devil under the weak light of the moon?"

    PRAY FOR YOUR DISKS!!"

After 2000 keystrokes the virus starts changing the colors of displayed text, after 5000 keystrokes it erases the first copy of the FAT. A Dance-B infected system will run very slowly.

Diabolik

>Aliases: Italian Pest, Pest, Murphy
>
>Spread: Research
>
>Infects: .EXE
>
>Length: 1910
>
>Internal message:
>
>"*.COM"
>
>"(c) by Cracker Jack 1991 Italian Virus Research Laboratory
>
>Created, Developed and Written by Cracker Jack,
>
>All rights reserved
>
>Con questo virus dichiaro guerra a tutti i POVERI
>
>(ahhh quanto sono poveri!)
>
>cosiddetti 'Virus Researchers' del globo...
>
>provate a prendermi..ahahahah
>
>l'IVRL e'forte.....vincera!!!!
>
>Virus Writers di tutte le nazioni...uniamci!"
>
>Symptoms: System boot failure, system hangs, program may disappear. Executing a .COM program displays I'm hungry!! Why don't you buy me a Cheeseburger??.
>
>On Fridays, activates and displays the message Your PC is infected with the Intergalactic Pest!, and then overwrites FAT and boot sector.

Dir-2

>Aliases: Creeping Death, FAT Virus
>
>Spread: Common
>
>Stealth: DIR-II: Multipartite, Accelerated Infector, Dissimulator, Polymorphic, Boot Survivor
>
>Infects: File Allocation Table (Directory Structure)

Length: n/a

Symptoms: CHKDSK results in lost clusters and program corruption on file copy.

Disk Killer (2)

Aliases: Computer Ogre, Disk Ogre, Ogre

Spread: Common

Infects: Boot sector

Length:

Symptoms: After virus has been live for 48 hours, it displays the following message:

Disk Killer—Version 1.00 by COMPUTER OGRE 04/01/89

Warning!!

Don't turn off the power or remove the diskette while

Disk Killer is Processing!

PROCESSING

Now you can turn off the power. I wish you Luck!"

and scrambles the disk.

Do Nothing 640k

Spread: Extinct

Infects: .COM

Length: 608

Symptoms: Replication only.

Doom-II/B (2)

Spread: Rare

Infects: .COM, .EXE

Length: 1252

Symptoms: System hangs on screen writes.

Dot Killer

> Aliases: 944, Point Killer, Dot Eater
>
> Spread: Rare
>
> Infects: .COM
>
> Length: 944
>
> Symptoms: Removes all dots (.) from display.

Durban Saturday 14th

> Spread: Rare
>
> Infects: .COM, .EXE, .OV?
>
> Length: 669
>
> Symptoms: On Saturday the 14th, the virus corrupts the boot sector, FAT, and partition table.

E.D.V. (2)

> Aliases: Cursy, Stealth Virus, EDV
>
> Spread: Common
>
> Infects: Boot sector and partition table
>
> Length:
>
> Internal Message: "MSDOS Vers. E.D.V."
>
> Symptoms: Partition table corruption, unusual system crashes. Overwrites the disk, and then displays `That rings a bell, no? From Cursy.`

Eight Tunes (6)

> Aliases: 1971
>
> Spread: Rare
>
> Infects: .COM, .EXE
>
> Length: 1971
>
> Symptoms: Plays eight German folk songs at random intervals.

Einstein

    Spread: Rare

    Infects: .EXE

    Length: 979 - 892

    Internal Message: "exeEXE" and "Einstein"

    Symptoms: Replicates only.

England

    Alias: Crazy Eddie

    Spread: New

    Infects: .COM, .EXE, partition table

    Length: 2600 - 2715

    Internal Message: "Crazy Eddie"

    Symptoms: Hard disk corruption and file allocation errors.

Evil Empire

    Spread: Common (stoned variant)

    Infects: Boot sector/partition table

    Length:

    Internal Massage: PC ♥ AT

    Symptoms: Replication only.

Evil/V1226 (3)

    Aliases: P1, V1701New, Live after Death 3

    Spread: Rare

    Infects: .COM

    Length: 1701

    Symptoms: System reboots, CHKDSK program failure, COMMAND.COM header change.

F-Word (2)

>   Alias: 417

>   Spread: Rare

>   Infects: .COM

>   Length: 417

>   Internal message: F _ _ _ You!

>   Symptoms: File date/time changes.

Father Christmas (2)

>   Alias: Choinka

>   Spread: Rare

>   Infects: .COM

>   Length: 1881

>   Symptoms: Lost cluster, cross-linking, graphic display of Christmas tree and the following message:

>   ```
>   Merry Christmas
>
>   &
>
>   a Happy New Year
>
>   for all my lovely friends
>
>   from
>
>   FATHER CHRISTMAS.
>   ```

Fellowship

>   Aliases: 1022, Better World

>   Spread: Rare

>   Infects: .EXE

>   Length: 1022

Internal Message:

"This message is dedicated to

all fellow PC users on Earth

Toward A Better Tomorrow

And a better Place To Live In"

"03/03/90 KV KL MAL"

Symptoms: Replication only.

Fish (9)

Aliases: European Fish Viruses, Fish 6, Stealth Virus

Stealth: Polymorphic

Spread: Rare

Infects: .COM, .EXE

Length: 3584

Internal Message: "FISK FI," several fish names randomly appear in virus TSR

Symptoms: Monitor/display flickering.

Flash

Spread: Rare

Infects: .COM, .EXE

Length: 688

Symptoms: Video screen flash every seven minutes.

Flip (6)

Aliases: Flip-2343, Flip-2153, Flip-2153B

Spread: Common

Infects: .COM, .EXE, overlay files, Partition Table

Length: 2343

Symptoms: File allocation errors and the EGA and VGA systems screen flips horizontally from 4 p.m. to 4:59 p.m.

Form

Aliases: FORM-Virus, Form Boot, FORM-18

Spread: Common

Infects: Boot sector

Length:

Internal message:

"The FORM-Virus sends greetings to everyone who's reading this text. FORM doesn't destroy data! Don't panic! F _ _ _ ings go to Corinne."

Symptoms: Clicking noise from speaker on 24th day of any month.

Friday 13th (2)

Aliases: COM virus, Miami, Munich, South Africa, 55512 Virus, Virus B

Spread: Extinct

Infects: .COM

Length: 512

Symptoms: Floppy =0disk access, infected programs deleted if executed on Friday the 13th.

Friday 13th-B

Spread: Extinct

Infects: every .COM file in current directory and path

Length: 512

Symptoms: Floppy-disk access, infected programs deleted if executed on Friday the 13th.

Fu Manchu (14)

Aliases: 2080, 2086, Fu-Manchu-B

Spread: Rare

Infects: .COM, .EXE, .BIN, .SYS, .OVL

Length: 2086 (.COM), 2080(.EXE)

Internal message: "sAXrEMHOr"

Symptoms: After Aug. 1, adds derogatory comments to the names of various politicians to the keyboard buffer.

Gergana (6)

Family of viruses: Gergana II, Gergana III, Gergana IV, Gergana-222, Gergana-300, Gergana-450, Gergana-512, Gergana-182B

Spread: Rare

Infects: .COM

Length: 182

Internal messages:

"Gergana V"

"For nice time call [359][032] 557-XXX." (number omitted for privacy)

"[Enter] to continue."

or

"*.COM," "GERGANA," "-IV Free," and

"This file is infected. Press [Enter] to continue."

Symptoms: File date/time changes.

Ghostballs (5)

Aliases: Ghost Boot, Ghost COM, Ghostballs.1

Spread: Extinct

Infects: .COM and boot sector (Ghostballs was the first virus capable of infecting files and boot sectors.)

Length: 2351

Internal Message:

"GhostBalls, Product of Iceland

Copyright (c) 1989, 4418 and 5F10

MSDOS 3.2"

Symptoms: File corruption, moving graphics display similar to ping pong.

GP1

Aliases: Jerusalem-GP, Get Password 1

Spread: Rare

Infects: .COM, .EXE on Novell Networks

Length: 1914

Symptoms: Attempts to capture Novell Netware passwords, and does not work properly.

Grapje

Aliases: 1023 + 27, 1039, Dutch 1039

Spread: Rare

Infects: .COM

Length: 1039

Internal Message:

"????????COM"

"*.com"

"GRAPJE!!"

Symptoms: Long program loads, system hangs, displays GRAPJE on the last day of the month, a split-second before midnight.

Gremlin

Alias: Alf

Spread: Rare

Infects: .COM, .EXE

Length:1146

Internal Message: "gremlin"

Symptoms: System slowdown, and file dates may disappear.

Guppy

> Alias: Guppy-B
>
> Spread: Rare
>
> Infects: .COM, .EXE
>
> Length: 152
>
> Internal Message: 3ECD211F5A5B58EA
>
> Symptoms: Disk boot failures and the `Invalid file or drive name` error message.

Haifa v1.01

> Spread: Common
>
> Infects: .COM
>
> Length: 2351 - 2372
>
> Symptoms: Possible system hangs when executing infected programs, file date/time change.

Halloechen (6)

> Spread: Rare
>
> Infects: .COM, .EXE
>
> Length: 2011
>
> Symptoms: Garbled keyboard input.

Hero

> Spread: Rare
>
> Infects: .COM, .EXE
>
> Length: 506
>
> Symptoms: System hangs and program corruption.

Horse (3)

> Stealth: Dissimulator
>
> Spread: Rare
>
> Infects: .COM, .EXE

Length: 1160

Internal Message: "Sofia,1991 (c) Naughty Hacker."

Symptoms: Buzzing sound effects, scrolling display makes clicking sound, and running CHKDSK/F will corrupt programs.

Horse Boot

Alias: Horse Boot Dropper, Stoned variant

Spread: Rare

Infects: Boot sector and partition table

Length:

Symptoms: High-density diskette corruption.

Hybrid

Alias: Hybryd

Spread: Rare

Infects: .COM

Length: 1306

Symptoms: Replications.

Hymn (2)

Spread: Rare

Infects: .COM, .EXE

Length: 1865 - 1883

Internal Messages: "ibm@SNS" and "@ussr@"

Symptoms: May play music.

Icelandic-1 (5)

Aliases: 656, One In Ten, Disk Crunching Virus, Saratoga 2

Spread: Extinct

Infects: every tenth .EXE

Length: 656

Symptoms: Bad sectors and FAT corruption.

Icelandic-2 (3)

    Aliases: System Virus, One in Ten

    Stealth: Accelerated Infector

    Spread: Extinct

    Infects: .EXE

    Length: 632

    Symptoms: FAT Corruption, date changes, and loss of read-only attributes.

Icelandic-3 (3)

    Alias: December 24th

    Spread: Endangered

    Infects: .EXE

    Length: 848-863

    Symptoms: FAT corruption, and on Dec. 24 displays `Gledileg jol` ("Merry Christmas" in Icelandic).

Incom

    Spread: Rare

    Infects: .COM

    Length: 648

    Internal Message: "INCOM."

    Symptoms: File date/time change

Invader (8)

    Aliases: Plastique Boot, Mozart, Sledge Hammer, Chinese Invader, Anticad 4

    Spread: Common

    Infects: .COM, .EXE and boot sector

    Length: 4096

    Internal Message: "PC Tools" (possible)

Symptoms: Plays music, usually a Mozart melody or theme song from TV show "Sledge Hammer."

Italian-A

Aliases: Ping Pong, Bouncing Ball, Boot, Bouncing Dot, Italian, Vera Cruz

Spread: Common

Infects: Boot sector

Length:

Symptoms: Bouncing ball or dot on screen. You must reboot to remove ball.

Italian-B

Aliases: Italian 803, Italian File, V817, Sept. 18, Italian 803-B

Spread: Rare

Infects: .COM, .EXE

Length: 803

Symptoms: Replication only.

ItaVir (2)

Alias: 3880

Spread: Endangered

Infects: .EXE

Length: 3880

Symptoms: Writes ANSI values from 0 to 255 to all available I/O ports. Some monitors may show a flickering effect.

Jabberwock

Aliases: JW2, 812, Jabberwocky

Spread: Rare

Infects: .COM, .EXE

Length: 812

Internal Message: "JW2"

Symptoms: Some variants may display BEWARE THE JABBERWOCK!.

Jerspain (4)

Aliases: Spanish JB, Jerusalem F, Jerusalem E2

Spread: Very Common

Infects: .COM, .EXE

Length: 1808

Internal Message: none

Symptoms: No Jerusalem black box. Deletes program on Friday the 13th.

Jerusalem

(see section on Jerusalem Virus in Chapter 2)

Aliases: PLO, Israeli, Friday the 13th, Russian, 1813(COM), 1808(EXE), Arab Star, Black Box, Black Widow, Hebrew University

Family of viruses: A-204, Anarkia, Anarkia-B, Antiviru, Apocalypse, Captain Trips, Captain Trips 2, Get Password, January 25th, January 25th-B, Jerusalem B, Jeru-C, Jeru-D, Jeru DC, Jeru-E, Jeru-PLO, JVT1, JVT1-B, Mendoza, Messina, Nemesis, New Jerusalem, Payday, Park ESS, Phenome, Puerto, Skism, Skism-1, Spanish-JB, Swiss 1813

Variants: 1605, Discom, Frere Jacques, Fu Manchu, Groen Links, Growing Blocks, Jeru-11-30, Jeru 1767, Mule, RAM Virus, Slow, Sunday, Sunday-2, Suriv 3.00, Westwood

Spread: Very Common

Infects: .COM, .EXE

Length: 1808 - 1822

Symptoms: Possible black box on lower left side of screen after 30 minutes, possible system slowdown, deletes infected programs that are executed on any Friday the 13th (some variants and strains change the day).

Jojo (3)

> Spread: Rare
>
> Infects: .COM
>
> Length: 1701
>
> Internal Messages: "Welcome to the JOJO Virus." and "F _ _ _ the system (c)-1990"
>
> Symptoms: Running second infected program will result in multicolored diamond screen display.

Joshi (3)

> Aliases: Happy Birthday Joshi, Stealth Virus
>
> Spread: Very Common
>
> Infects: Boot sector and partition table
>
> Length:
>
> Symptoms: On Jan. 5th displays message type `"Happy Birthday Joshi" if you enter "Happy Birthday Joshi" the system can continue.`

July 13th

> Spread: Endangered
>
> Infects: .EXE
>
> Length: 1201
>
> Symptoms: On July 13th a bouncing ball effect similar to the Italian Ping Pong virus.

June 16 (3)

> Spread: Endangered
>
> Infects: .COM
>
> Length: 879
>
> Symptoms: Long disk access, on June 16 the FAT is altered, all entries changed to "ZAPPED."

Kamikaze

> Spread: Endangered
>
> Infects: .EXE
>
> Length: 4031
>
> Internal Message: "kamikazi"
>
> Symptoms: System hangs and reboots.

Kennedy

> Aliases: Dead Kennedy, 333, Kenedy-333
>
> Spread: Endangered
>
> Infects: .COM
>
> Length: 333
>
> Symptoms: Cross-linking of files, lost clusters, and file allocation table errors. There are three activation dates:
>
> June 6, assassination of Robert Kennedy 1968
>
> November 18, death of Joseph Kennedy 1969
>
> November 22, assassination of President John F. Kennedy
>
> On any of these three dates, the virus displays `Kennedy is dead—long live 'The Dead Kennedys.'`

Keydrop

> Alias: Keydrop Dropper
>
> Spread: Rare
>
> Infects: Boot sector and partition table
>
> Length:
>
> Symptoms: Characters dropped from keyboard buffer, possible file damage.

Keypress (5)

> Spread: Common
>
> Infects: .COM, .EXE

Length: 1239

Symptoms: Keystrokes repeated unexpectedly.

Kiev

Aliases: Kiev 483, 483

Spread: Rare

Infects: .COM

Length: 483

Internal Messages:

"Kiev 1990"

"????????COM"

"*.COM"

Symptoms: Replication only.

Klaeren

Alias: Hate

Stealth: Polymorphic

Spread: Rare

Infects: .COM, .EXE

Length: 978

Symptoms: System slowdown.

Korea LBC

Aliases: Korea, LBC Boot

Spread: Common - Korea

Infects: Floppy boot sectors

Length:

Symptoms: Possible directory errors on 360Kb diskettes.

Label

Alias: Int13

Stealth: Accelerated Infector

Spread: Rare

Infects: .COM

Length: 512 (overwrites)

Symptoms: Program corrupted as it is overwritten with virus, sluggish DIS commands, and `sector not found` errors.

Leapfrog

Aliases: USSR 516, V516, 516

Spread: Rare (research)

Infects: .COM

Length: 516

Symptoms: Replication.

Leech (3)

Aliases: Leech2, Topler

Spread: Rare

Infects: .COM

Length: 1024

Symptoms: File dates may disappear.

Lehigh

Alias: Lehigh University

Spread: Common

Infects: Overwrites COMMAND.COM

Length:

Symptoms: After four or ten (depending on variant) it will corrupt the boot sector and FAT, .EXE files may result in system hang.

Leprosy

Alias: News Flash

Family of Viruses: Leprosy-A, Leprosy-B, Leprosy-C, Leprosy-D

Spread: Rare

Infects: .COM, .EXE

Length: 666, 320, or 370

Symptoms: Program corruption, may display one of the following messages:

```
"Program too big to fit in memory"
"NEWS FLASH!! Your system has been infected with the
 incurable decay of LEPROSY 1.00, a virus invented by
 PCM2 in June of 1990. Good luck!"
"Bad or missing Command Interpreter".
```

Liberty

Family of Viruses: Liberty A through J

Stealth: Polymorphic

Spread: Common

Infects: .COM, .EXE, .OVL

Length: 2859 - 2873

Internal messages:

"- M Y S T I C - COPYRIGHT (C) 1989-2000, by SsAsMsUsEsL" and "Magic"

Symptoms: File date/time changes.

Lisbon-A/B (11)

Spread: Rare

Infects: .COM

Length: 648

Internal Messages: "@AIDS," and "????????COM"

Symptoms: Infected programs are corrupted and will hang the system.

Lozinsky (2)

> Aliases: Lozinsky-1018, Lozinski-1023B, Zherkov
>
> Spread: Rare
>
> Infects: .COM
>
> Length: 1023
>
> Symptoms: File date/time change.

Magnitogorsk (2)

> Stealth: Dissimulator
>
> Alias: Magnitogorsk 2048
>
> Spread: Rare
>
> Infects: .COM, .EXE
>
> Length: 2048
>
> Symptoms:

Maltese Amoeba

> Aliases: Amoeba, Irish
>
> Spread: Common
>
> Infects: .COM, .EXE
>
> Length: 2504 - 2564
>
> Internal Hidden Message:
>
> "AMOEBA virus by the Hacker Twins (C) 1991
>
> This is nothing, wait for the release of AMOEBA II -
>
> The universal infector, hidden to any eye by ours!
>
> Dedicated to the University of Malta-the worst
>
> of 5X2 years of human life".
>
> Symptoms: On March 15 or November 1 it will effectively over-write the hard disk and display the message:

```
To see a world in a grain of sand,

And a heaven in a flower

Hold infinity in the palm of your hand

And eternity in an hour.

THE VIRUS 16/3/91.
```

Mardi Bros (2)

Spread: Rare

Infects: Floppy boot sector

Length:

Internal Message: "Sudah ada vaksin"

Symptoms: Diskette volume label change to "Mardi Bros."

Mendoza (2)

Family: Jerusalem-B variant

Spread: Common

Infects: .COM, .EXE (does not reinfect .EXE files)

Length: 1808

Symptoms: No black box during second half of the year (July - December). There is a 10% chance that any infected program executed will be deleted.

MG-1

Family: MG-2, MG-3, MG-31

Spread: Rare

Infects: .COM

Length: 500

Symptoms: DIR command may not function properly, file allocation errors, system hangs.

MGTU (2)

Spread: Rare

Infects: .COM

Length: 273

Symptoms: Excessive disk activity, file date/time change, and the ????????COM Path not found message.

Michelangelo (see discussion on Michelangelo in Chapter 1 and Chapter 2)

Spread: Very Common

Infects: Boot sector and partition table

Length: system memory decrease of 2048 bytes

Symptoms: On March 6th it will format the hard disk by over-writing it with random characters.

Microbes (2)

Spread: Common

Infects: Floppy boot sector

Length:

Symptoms: System may hang during boot.

Miky

Spread: Rare

Infects: .COM, .EXE

Length: 2350

Symptoms: One lost cluster each time Miky is executed, random activation, screen rotation to the right and message MIKY 786290 B♥livia.

Mini-45

Family of viruses: Minimal, Short-45, Mini-45, Mini-44, Mini-46, Mini-97, Mini-99

Spread: Research

Infects: .COM

Length: 45

Symptoms: File date/time changes.

Mix-1 (8)

Spread: Rare

Infects: .EXE

Length: 1618

Internal Message: "MIX1"

Symptoms: Serial and parallel port garbled output, Num Lock always on. After the 6th infection, booting the system will crash the system and a bouncing ball will appear.

Mix-2

Spread: Rare

Infects: .COM, .EXE

Length: 2287

Symptoms: Possible system hang when running infected programs.

Murphy 1/2 (2)

Spread: Common

Infects: .COM, .EXE

Length: 1277

Internal Message:

"Hello, I'm Murphy. Nice to meet you friend.

I'm written since Nov./Dec.

Copywrite (c)1989 by Lubo & Ian, Sofia, USM Laboratory."

Symptoms: Speaker noise.

Murphy(2) (2)

Spread: Rare

Infects: .COM, .EXE

Length: 1521

Internal Message:

"It's me—Murphy.

Copywrite (c)1990 by Lubo & Ian, Sofia, USM Laboratory."

Symptoms: Possible bouncing ball effect.

Music Bug (3)

Alias: Music Boot

Spread: Common

Infects: Boot sector and partition table

Length:

Internal Message:

"MusicBug v1.06. MacroSoft Corp."

"Made in Taiwan"

Symptoms: Plays music when booting and randomly during disk access.

Mutant (3)

Family of viruses: Mutant 123, Mutant 127, Mutant 128, Tiny Mutant, Tiny-123, Tiny-127

Spread: Rare

Infects: .COM

Length: 123 - 128

Symptoms: .COM file corruption, disk boot failure, file date/time changes, system hangs.

Naughty Hacker-1 (4)

Family of viruses: Naughty Hacker A through Naughty G, Horse

Stealth: Dissimulator

Spread: Rare

Infects: .COM, .EXE

Length: 1154 or 1160

Symptoms: File allocation errors, buzzing from system speaker, and clicking.

Nina (3)

Spread: Rare

Infects: .COM

Length: 256

Internal Message: "Nina"

Symptoms: Virus replication only.

Nomenklatura

Aliases: Nomenclature, 1024-B

Spread: Common

Infects: .COM, .EXE

Length: 1024

Internal Message: "Nomenklatura"

Symptoms: `sector not found` error on diskettes.

Off Stealth (2)

Aliases: SVC 4.0, USSR 1689, SVC V4.0, SVC 4.0-1740

Spread: Rare

Infects: .COM, .EXE

Length: 1689

Symptoms: System hangs and file allocation errors.

Ohio

Alias: (may be identified as Den Zuk)

Spread: Common

Infects: Floppy boot sector

Length:

Internal Message:

"V I R U S

b y

The Hackers

Y C 1 E R P

D E N Z U K 0

Bandung 40254

Indonesia

(C) 1988, The Hackers Team...."

Symptoms: Replication only.

Ontario

Spread: Common

Infects: .COM, .EXE

Length: 512

Symptoms: Possible hard disk errors over time.

Oropax (3)

Aliases: Music Virus, Musician

Spread: Rare

Infects: .COM

Length: 2756 - 2806 (usually 2773)

Symptoms: Plays three or six different tunes (depending on strain) every seven minutes.

Paris

Spread: Rare

Infects: .COM, .EXE

Length: 4909

Symptoms: Slow program loads upon execution, and diskette corruption after diskette boot.

Parity (2)

> Spread: Rare
>
> Infects: .COM
>
> Length: 441
>
> Symptoms: Long .COM program loads, randomly displays message PARITY CHECK 2 and halts system.

Pentagon

> Spread: Extinct
>
> Stealth: Boot Survivor
>
> Infects: Diskette boot sector
>
> Length:
>
> Symptoms: Creates two files: 0F9(hex) and PENTAGON.TXT, and changes IBM to HAL in the boot sector.

Perfume (6)

> Aliases: 765, 4711, G-Virus
>
> Spread: Common
>
> Infects: .COM
>
> Length: 765
>
> Symptoms: Asks question in German, correct answer "4711"— a German perfume. The question has been overwritten with random characters in the most common variant of this virus.

Pixel (8)

> Aliases: V-345
>
> Spread: Endangered
>
> Infects: .COM
>
> Length: 345

Internal Message:

"*.COM"

"=!= Program sick error: Call doctor or buy Pixel for cure

description"

"WB"

or

"*.COM"

"F _ _ _ng hell: You wet p _ _ _ _"

or

"*.COM"

"=!What a stupid you are !!!!!!!!"

or

"=!= I love you so much !!!"

"— Francis"

"*.COM"

or

"=!= En tu PC hay un virus RV1, y esta es su quinta generacion."

Symptoms: Replication only.

Plague

Alias: The Plague

Spread: Rare

Infects: .COM, .EXE

Length: 590

Symptoms: `Program too big to fit in memory` error message,
long disk accesses. When all programs are infected the following
message appears:

`Autopsy indicates the cause of`

`death was THE PLAGUE`

`Dedicated to the dudes at SHHS`

```
VIVE LE SHE-MAN!"
```

and overwrites the hard disk unrecoverably.

Plastique (7)

> Aliases: Plastic Bomb, PLastique 3012, Anticad 3
>
> Spread: Rare
>
> Infects: .COM, .EXE
>
> Length: 3012
>
> Symptoms: Possible system slowdown and "bomb" noises after Sept. 20.

Plastique 5.21 (6)

> Spread: Rare
>
> Infects: .COM, .EXE
>
> Length: 4096
>
> Symptoms: Possible system slowdown and "bomb" noises after Sept. 20. Also may overwrite the hard disk.

Plastique-2 (9)

> Spread: Rare
>
> Infects: .COM, .EXE
>
> Length: 4096
>
> Symptoms:

Polimer

> Alias: Polimer Tapeworm
>
> Spread: Rare
>
> Infects: .COM
>
> Length: 512
>
> Symptoms: Displays message, A le' jobb kazetta a POLIMER kazetta ! Vegye ezt !.

Polish 217

> Aliases: 217, Polish Stupid, V217
>
> Spread: Rare
>
> Infects: .COM
>
> Length: 217
>
> Symptoms: Executes an infected COMMAND.COM and reboots the system.

Possessed

> Family of Viruses: Possesed-2442, Possessed 1.03A, Possessed 1.03B, Possessed 1.07, Possessed 1.08
>
> Spread: Rare
>
> Infects: .COM, .EXE
>
> Length: 2446 - 2460
>
> Symptoms: Programs disappear, and writes fault errors on COM1.

Print Screen (2)

> Aliases: EB 21 8290, PRTSC Virus
>
> Spread: Common
>
> Infects: Boot sector
>
> Length:
>
> Symptoms: Hard disk access slowdown.

PS-Stoned

> Spread: Very Common
>
> Infects: Boot sector and partition table
>
> Length:
>
> Symptoms: Mo message, no display, and almost invisible except for replication.

PSQR-A (2)

> Alias: 1720 (Jerusalem variant)
>
> Spread: Rare
>
> Infects: .COM, .EXE
>
> Length: 1719 - 1733
>
> Symptoms: Partition-table damage. Programs deleted on Friday the 13th.

RaubKopie (2)

> Spread: Rare
>
> Infects: .COM, .EXE
>
> Length: 2219
>
> Symptoms: Displays the following message:

```
A  C  H  T  U  N  G

- - - - - - - - - - - - - - - - - - - - - - - - -

Die Benutzung einer RAUBKOPIE ist strafbar!

Nur wer Original-Disketten, Handbucher,

oder PD-Lizenzen besitzt, darf Kopien verwenden.

Programmierung is muhevolle Detailarbeit:

Wer Raubkopien verwendet, betrugt

Programmierer un den Lohn ihrer Arbeit.

- - - - - - - - - - - - - - - - - - - - - - - - -
```

It then pauses and asks:

```
Bist Du sauber ? (J/N)
```

Answering "J" results in `Ich will glauben, was Du sagst`
`.....`

Answering "N" results in a terminated program and `CPU-ID wird gespeichert...`

```
**** LO<garbled>   "
```

```
**** Losche dieses Programm ****
```

Red-Diavolyata (3)

    Aliases: USSR 830, MLTI

    Spread: Rare

    Infects: .COM

    Length: 830

    Internal Message:

    "Eddie die somewhere in time"

    "This programm was written in the city of Prostokwashino"

    "(C) 1990 RED DIAVOLYATA"

    "Hello! MLTI!"

    Symptoms: File date/time changes.

Rostov

    Spread: Common (Stoned variant)

    Infects: Boot sector and partition table

    Length:

    Internal Messages: "Replace and strike" and "Non-system disk"

    Symptoms: No message displayed.

Saddam

    Alias: Professor

    Spread: Rare

    Infects: .COM

    Length: 919

    Symptoms: Disk boot failures, I/O error message, running .BAT file results in `Insufficient memory` message, *DIR command* error, system hangs and then displays

    `HEY SADAM`

    `LEAVE QUIET BEFORE I COME.`

Saratoga (3)

> Aliases: 764, One in Two
>
> Stealth: Accelerated Infector
>
> Spread: Extinct
>
> Infects: .EXE
>
> Length: 642
>
> Symptoms: Bad sector and FAT corruption.

Saturday the 14th (2)

> Alias: Durban
>
> Spread: Rare
>
> Infects: .COM, .EXE, .OV?
>
> Length: 669
>
> Symptoms: On Saturday the 14th, the boot sector, FAT table and partition table are corrupted.

Scotts Valley

> Aliases: 2131, Slow-2131
>
> Spread: Rare
>
> Infects: .COM, .EXE
>
> Length: 2131
>
> Symptoms: Replication only.

Self-457

> Alias: Polish-457
>
> Spread: Rare
>
> Infects: .COM
>
> Length: 457
>
> Possible Internal Messages: "MS *.COM" or "RZRZ"
>
> Symptoms: File date/time change.

Self-550

> Alias: Polish-550
>
> Spread: Rare
>
> Infects: .COM
>
> Length: 500
>
> Internal Messages: "CMS*.COM," "*.EXE," and "QYQY"
>
> Symptoms: File date/time changes.

Sentinel (3)

> Aliases: Sentinal-3, Sentianal-5, BC
>
> Spread: Rare
>
> Infects: .COM, .EXE
>
> Length: 4625
>
> Internal Messages:
>
> "You won't hear me, but you'll feel me....
>
> (c) 1990 by Sentinel.
>
> With thanks to Borland."
>
> Symptoms: System hangs and Keyboard stuck key failure appears.

Shake (4)

> Alias: Shake Dropper
>
> Spread: Rare
>
> Infects: .COM
>
> Length: 476
>
> Symptoms: Randomly displays message Shake well before use! when attempting to run an infected program.

Slow (6)

> Aliases: Slowdown, Zerotime
>
> Spread: Common

Infects: .COM, .EXE

Length: 1701

Symptoms: Some infected .EXE program may hang the system.

Solano (3)

Aliases: Solano 2000, Dyslexia 2.01

Spread: Rare

Infects: .COM

Length: 2000

Symptoms: Occasionally transposes numbers on the screen.

Sorry (2)

Aliases: G-Virus V1.3, Perfume-2

Spread: Rare

Infects: .COM

Length: 731

Internal Message:

"G-VIRUS V1.3"

"Bitte gebe den G-Virus Code ein"

"Tit mir Leid !"

Symptoms: Replication only.

Spanish Telecom

Aliases: Telfonica, Telecom File, Spanish Telecom-2

Spread: Common

Infects: .COM and partition table

Length: 3700

Symptoms: Hard disk formats on the 400th boot.

Spyer

>Aliases: Faust, Spyer-B, Spyer-C
>
>Spread: Rare
>
>Infects: .COM, .EXE
>
>Length: 1181
>
>Symptoms: System hangs when attempting to reinfect a program.

STAF

>Alias: Staff
>
>Spread: Rare
>
>Infects: .COM
>
>Length: 2083
>
>Symptoms: Program may fail to execute. When a program is infected, Staf displays the following message:

```
This program has been infected by:

Virus Demo Ver.: 1.1 - Handle with care!

By STAF (Tel.: (819) 595-0787)

Generation #n

Infecting: xxxxxxxx.COM

Press any key to execute original program...
```

>If all the programs have been infected Staf displays:

```
I have infected all your files in the current
directory!

Have a nice day!
```

Star Dot

>Aliases: StarDot 600, StarDot 789, StarDot 801
>
>Spread: Common

Infects: .EXE

Length: 604

Symptoms: Hard disk corruption, random characters to I/O ports, system hangs.

Stoned (13) (see section on Stoned virus in Chapter 2)

Aliases: Donald Duck, Hawaii, Marijuana, New Zealand, Rostov, San Diego, Sex Revolution, Smithsonian, Stoned II, Deunis

Spread: The Most Common Virus

Infects: Boot sector and partition table

Length:

Symptoms: Upon booting, randomly displays a message similar to Your PC is now Stoned!.

Subliminal

Spread: Rare

Infects: .COM

Length: 1496

Symptoms: Unusual file errors and video display flicker as the virus flashes LOVE, REMEMBER? in the lower-left portion of the display as a subliminal message.

Sunday (22)

Spread: Common

Infects: .COM, .EXE, .OV?

Length: 1636

Symptoms: FAT corruption, and the following message on any Sunday:

Today is Sunday! Why do you work so hard?

All work and no play make you a dull boy!

Come on! Let's go out and have some fun!

Sunday-2

Spread: Rare

Infects: .COM, .EXE

Length: 2877

Symptoms: File allocation errors, system hangs and the following message on any Sunday:

```
It's Sunday. Why are you working?

Take the day off compliments of RABID.
```

Suriv-1 (6)

Aliases: April 1st, Israeli, Suriv01

Spread: Extinct

Infects: .COM

Length: 897

Internal Message: "sURIV 1.01"

Symptoms: System locks on April 1st after the following message is displayed:

```
APRIL 1ST HA HA HA YOU HAVE A VIRUS.
```

Suriv-2 (7)

Aliases: April 1st-B, Israeli

Spread: Extinct

Infects: .EXE

Length: 1488

Symptoms: System locks on April 1st after the following message is displayed:

```
APRIL 1ST HA HA HA YOU HAVE A VIRUS
```

Also will lock after one hour if system data is default: 1-1-80.

SVC v5.00

> Alias: USSR 3103
>
> Stealth: Dissimulator
>
> Spread: Common
>
> Infects: .COM, .EXE
>
> Length: 3103
>
> Internal Message: "(c) 1990 by SVC, Vers. 5.0"
>
> Symptoms: Program corruption.

Sverdlov (2)

> Alias: Hymn-2
>
> Stealth: Polymorphic
>
> Spread: Rare
>
> Infects: .COM, .EXE
>
> Length: 1962
>
> Symptoms: Replication only.

SVIR (5)

> Spread: Endangered
>
> Infects: .EXE
>
> Length: 512
>
> Symptoms: File date/time changed to date/time of infection, system hangs as virus may go into endless loop looking for a program to infect.

Swedish Disaster

> Spread: Rare
>
> Infects: Boot sector and partition table
>
> Length:
>
> Internal Message: "The Swedish Disaster"
>
> Symptoms: None

Sylvia (5)

> Alias: Holland Girl
>
> Spread: Rare
>
> Infects: .COM
>
> Length: 1332
>
> Internal Message: Lists address of girl in Holland
>
> Symptoms: Replication only.

Sylvia-A

> Alias: Holland Girl 2
>
> Spread: Rare
>
> Infects: .COM
>
> Length: 1332
>
> Internal Message: Lists address of girl in Holland
>
> Symptoms: Replication only.

Taiwan (5)

> Family of viruses: Taiwan 2, Doom I, Doom I-B
>
> Spread: Endangered
>
> Infects: .COM
>
> Length: 743
>
> Symptoms: Eighth day of any month, virus overwrites the FATs and the root directory.

Taiwan-3 (4)

> Spread: Common
>
> Infects: .COM, .EXE
>
> Length: 2900
>
> Symptoms: Replication only.

Taiwan-4 (6)

Aliases: 2576, Anticad 5

Spread: Common

Infects: .COM, .EXE

Length: 2576

Symptoms: System slows down after 30 minutes.

Tequila (12)

Alias: Stealth

Stealth: Polymorphic

Spread: Common

Infects: .EXE and partition table

Length: 2468

Hidden Message: "Welcome to T.TEQUILA's latest production.

Contact T.TEQUILA/P.o.Box 543/6312 St'hausen

Switzerland.

Loving thought to L.I.N.D.A.

BEER and TEQUILA forever !"

Symptoms: File allocation errors, may display `Execute: mov ax,`
`FE03 / int 21. Key to go on!.`

TestVirus B V1.4

Aliases: Tester, TestVir

Spread: Rare

Infects: .COM

Length: 1000

Symptoms: Displays the following message when executing infected program:

`This is TESTVIRUS B V1.4 !`

`1 = infect COM-files of this directory + run orig.prog.`

```
5 = run only orig. program

9 = abort
```

The response determines if the virus loads into memory.

Time-B

Aliases: Monxla B, Vienna 535

Spread: Rare

Infects: .COM

Length: 535

Symptoms: File corruption.

Tiny (2)

Aliases: Tiny Di-94, Tiny Di-101, Tiny Di 108, Tiny Di-110, Di-94, Di-101, Di08, Di-110

Spread: New

Infects: .COM

Length: 94 - 110

Symptoms: File date/time change, boot failure, and program corruption.

Tiny-Family (2)

Family of viruses: Tiny- 133, 134, 138, 143, 154, 156, 158, 160, 167, 198

Spread: Rare

Infects: .COM

Length: as per virus name

Symptoms: Virus replication only.

Topo

Spread: Rare

Infects: .EXE

Length: 1542 - 1552

Internal Message:

"COMSPEC=C:\DOS\COMMAND.COM PATH=C:\DOS"

"PHORSEFAX"

Symptoms: Possible write-protect errors.

TP33 family

Alias: Vacsina, TPxx

Family: TP33, TP34, TP38, TP41, TP42, TP45, TP46

Spread: Common

Infects: .COM and .EXE

Length: 1206

Symptoms: Some versions play "Yankee Doodle."

Tumen V.5

Spread: Rare

Infects: .COM

Length: 1663

Internal Message:

"Full moon tonight... The time of Wolfbacks... U...U...U...

This is only demonstration version, but you hear some howl."

"(C) Copyright MMA Company

All rights reserved. USSR Tumen 1990-v0.5

This program was created in Tumen by group of

three Wolfbacks at April,1990

General System_&_Files affecting effects by Max

Main consultant — Tall Lazy Micle

General Music_&_Video harmless effects by Alex

BACKWOLFS OF THE WORLD, UNITE!!"

Symptoms: File date/time changes, music, graphics.

Tumen V2.0

   Spread: Rare

   Infects: .COM

   Length: 1092

   Symptoms: System hangs and file date/time change.

Twin-351

   Spread: Rare

   Stealth: Multipartite Infector, Dissimulator

   Infects: .COM, .EXE

   Length: 351

   Symptoms: .COM file created with system and hidden attributes.

Typo (4)

   Aliases: Fumble, 867, Type, 712, Typo-712

   Spread: Extinct

   Infects: .COM on even numbered days

   Length: 867

   Symptoms: Garbled printout.

Typo Boot

   Alias: Mistake

   Spread: Rare

   Infects: Boot sector

   Length:

   Symptoms: Garbled printout.

USSR

   Stealth: Polymorphic

   Spread: Rare

   Infects: .EXE

   Length: 576

Symptoms: Long program loads, system hangs, and boot sector and partition table damage.

USSR-257 (3)

Aliases: Kemerovo-B, V257

Spread: Rare

Infects: .COM

Length: 257

Symptoms: `Path not found` error messages, and file date/time changes.

USSR-394 (2)

Alias: Attention

Spread: Rare

Infects: .COM

Length: 394

Symptoms: Clicking sound from speaker on KeyPress, file date/time changes.

USSR-600 (2)

Alias: V600

Spread: Rare

Infects: .COM

Length: 600

Symptoms: Replication only.

USSR-711 (2)

Spread: Rare

Infects: .COM

Length: 711

Symptoms: Possible system hangs.

USSR-948 (2)

>Alias: V948

>Spread: Rare

>Infects: .COM, .EXE

>Length: 948

>Symptoms: Replication only.

USSR2144

>Alias: V2144

>Spread: Rare

>Infects: .COM, .EXE

>Length: 2144

>Symptoms: Replication only.

V200

>Aliases: Silly Virus, 200

>Spread: Rare

>Infects: .COM

>Length: 200

>Symptoms: File date/time changes.

V651 (2)

>Aliases: Eddie 3, Stealth Virus, Dark Avenger 2

>Spread: Rare

>Infects: .COM, .EXE

>Length: 651

>Internal Message: "Eddie Lives!"

>Symptoms: File allocation errors.

V800 (4)

> Alias: Live after Death
>
> Spread: Rare
>
> Infects: .COM
>
> Length: 800
>
> Symptoms: Replication only.

V1024 (5)

> Aliases: Dark Avenger III, Stealth Virus, Diamond, 1024
>
> Stealth: Dissimulator
>
> Spread: Rare
>
> Infects: .COM, .EXE
>
> Length: 1024
>
> Internal Message: 7106286813
>
> Symptoms: Replication only.

V2000 (2)

> Alias: Dark Avenger II, Stealth Virus, Travel Virus, Eddie 2000, Apocalypse II
>
> Spread: Rare
>
> Infects: .COM, .EXE, .OV?
>
> Length: 2000
>
> Internal Message:
>
> "Zopy me - I want to travel"
>
> "Copy me - I want to travel"
>
> Symptoms: Crashes, running CHKDSK may result in cross-linked files.

V2100

> Aliases: 2100, Stealth Virus, UScan Virus, Dark Avenger 4
>
> Spread: Rare
>
> Infects: .COM, .EXE
>
> Length: 2100
>
> Symptoms: File allocation errors, CHKDSK resulting in cross-linking of files.

V2P2/1260/Casper (18)

> Aliases: Chameleon
>
> Spread: Research
>
> Infects: .COM
>
> Length: 1426 - 2157
>
> Symptoms: Replication only.

V2P6(Z) (4)

> Spread: Research
>
> Stealth: Polymorphic
>
> Infects: .COM
>
> Length: 1946 - 2111
>
> Symptoms: Replication and possible message:

> ```
> "Hi! I'm Casper The Virus, And On April 1st I'm Gonna
>  F _ _ _ Up Your Hard Disk REAL BAD! In Fact It Might
> Just Be Impossible To Recover! How's That Grab Ya!
> <GRIN>"
> ```

> On April 1st, strains of this virus may destroy the first track of the hard disk.

Vacsina (8)

> Spread: Common

Infects: .COM, .EXE, .BIN, .SYS

Length: 1206

Symptoms: Plays "Yankee Doodle."

VComm (3)

Aliases: 637, Vienna 637

Spread: Rare

Infects: .EXE

Length: 637

Symptoms: Disk write failures.

VHP-348

Family of viruses: VHP- 348, 353, 367, 435, 757, 776

Spread: Research

Infects: .COM, (some variants: .EXE)

Length: 348 - 435

Symptoms: Possible system hangs.

Victor (3)

Spread: Rare

Infects: .COM, .EXE

Length: 2443 - 2458

Internal Message:

"Victor V1.0 The Incredible High Performance Virus

Enhanced versions available soon.

This program was imported from USSR.

Thanks to Ivan."

Symptoms: Data file corruption, file linking errors, random reboots.

Vienna (11)

> Aliases: Austrian, Unesco, DOS-62, DOS-68, 1 in 8, 648
>
> Family of viruses: Vienna-582, Vienna-B, Vienna-C
>
> Spread: Common
>
> Infects: .COM (1 in 6 files)
>
> Length: 648
>
> Symptoms: System reboots, system hangs, file time seconds changed to "62."

Violator B3

> Alias: Violator Strain B
>
> Spread: Endangered
>
> Infects: .COM
>
> Length: 1055
>
> Internal Message:
>
> "TransMogrified (TM) 1990 by
>
> RABID N'tnl Development Corp
>
> Copyright (c) 1990 RABID!
>
> Activation Date: 08/15/90
>
> - Violator Strain B -
>
> ! (Field Demo Test Version) !
>
> ! * NOT TO BE DISTRIBUTED * !"
>
> Symptoms: Formats drives, sector not found error on drive B:.

Virus-90 (5)

> Spread: Research
>
> Infects: .COM
>
> Length: 857
>
> Virus Author Notice:
>
> "This educational, research virus was written by
>
> Patrick Toulme to aid developers in understanding

direct-virus action and in creating virus-resistant software. This virus is a simple COM infector that will not infect a hard drive and advises the user when a file on a floppy disk is to be infected. Of course, no damage occurs from the virus and all infected files advise the user of the infection upon execution. The safeguards provided by the author prevent accidental infection and the disassembly of the code is extremely difficult. Upon request from the anti-viral community, Virus-90 is now only available to approved anti-virus researchers.

Symptoms: Replication

Virus-101 (6)

Spread: Research

Stealth: Polymorphic

Infects: All executable files, .COM, .EXE, boot sector

Length: 2560

Notice from Virus Author:

"Virus-101 is a sophisticated, continually encrypting, research virus written by Patrick Toulme, author of Virus-90. Virus-101 infects both COM and EXE files and will evade most anti-virus software and will continually encrypt itself to prevent non-algorithmic search scans.This virus is not available to the general public and is presently used by government agencies and corporate security departments to test anti-virus software and hardware devices."

Symptoms: Replication

Voronezh 2.01 (4)

>Aliases: Voronezh-Chemist, Chemist
>
>Spread: New
>
>Infects: .COM, .EXE
>
>Length: 650
>
>Internal Message:
>
>"Video mode 80x25 not supported"
>
>"16.01.91, v1.00"
>
>Symptoms: Replication.

VP (3)

>Spread: Rare
>
>Infects: .COM
>
>Length: 913
>
>Symptoms: System slowdown.

Vriest

>Spread: Rare
>
>Infects: .COM
>
>Length: 1280
>
>Symptoms: Replication.

W-13 A/B (9)

>Spread: Endangered
>
>Infects: .COM
>
>Length: 534
>
>Possible Internal Messages:
>
>"????????.com"
>
>"????????COM"

"REQ ! Ltd (c) 18:41:22 3-I-1991"

Symptoms: Replication.

Westwood (3)

Alias: improved Jerusalem variant

Spread: Rare

Infects: .COM, .EXE, .OVL

Length: 1819 - 1829

Symptoms: Black window, system slowdown, program deletion on Friday the 13th.

Whale-X

Aliases: Mother Fish, Stealth Virus, Z the Whale

Stealth: Polymorphic, Dissimulator

Spread: Research

Infects: .COM, .EXE

Length: 9216

Message in TSR: "Z the Whale"

Hidden Message in Root Directory:

```
"Fish Virus #9
A Whale is no Fish!
Mind her Mutant Fish
and the hidden Fish Eggs
for they are damaging.
The sixth Fish mutates
only if the Whale is in
her Cave."
```

Symptoms: System slowdown, video flicker, slow system screen writes, file allocation errors, simulated system reboot.

Wisconsin

> Alias: Death to Pascal
>
> Spread: Rare
>
> Infects: .COM
>
> Length: 825
>
> Symptoms: Write-protect errors, .PAS files disappear, file date/time changes, infected program may display `Death to Pascal`.

Wolfman (2)

> Spread: Rare
>
> Infects: .COM, .EXE
>
> Length: 2064
>
> Symptoms: Replication.

Yale/Alameda (4)

> Aliases: 500, Alameda, Mazatlan, Meritt, Peking, Seoul, Yale, Golden Gate, SF Virus
>
> Stealth: Boot Survivor
>
> Spread: Common
>
> Infects: Floppy boot sector
>
> Length:
>
> Symptoms: Floppy boot failures, most variants only infect diskettes.

Yankee-2

> Aliases: Yankee Virus, Yankee-go-Home, 1961, Old Yankee
>
> Spread: Endangered
>
> Infects: .EXE
>
> Length: 1961
>
> Symptoms: Plays "Yankee Doodle Dandy."

Zero-Bug (3)

    Aliases: Palette, 1536

    Spread: Endangered

    Infects: .COM

    Length: 1536

    Symptoms: Smiley face character appears and eats all the zeros on the screen.

Zero-Hunt (B)

    Aliases: Monnow, Stealth

    Stealth: Disinfector

    Spread: Research

    Infects: .COM

    Length: 416

    Symptoms: Replication only.

As this text was going to press the NAV Virus Definition Lab released the virus signatures for the following new viruses:

    644 (2)

    707

    733

    905 (2)

    Agiplan

    Beeper (2)

    Bhaktivedanta

    Black Monday (4)

    CheckFile Trojan

    Commfix Trojan

    Curse

    Ha Virus

Happy Day (2)

HeadCrash

Justice

Kylie

Lost Child

Lovechild

Lovechild Trojan

NumLock

Taiwan-5

Taiwan-6

TrackSwap

Trojan-17

Unknown Yankee Doodle

USSR-256 (2)

USSR-696 (2)

Vacsina-2

Vendetta

Warpcom (2)

Yankee-3

Glossary of Viral Terms

.COM—The file extension of an executable file. On the disk, a .COM file is the same size as when the file is being executed in memory.

.EXE—The file extension of an executable file that expands as it loads into memory.

Activation—When referring to a virus, activation has two meanings: when the virus becomes active in memory and when the virus is "triggered" and causes damage.

Assembly Language—A low-level programming, at the machine code level, assembly language provides virus programmers the most control over the operating systems and the application program.

Backdoor—A secret password or parameter that allows the programmer to activate undocumented features or bypass security

BBS—An electronic bulletin board connected to a modem. There are thousands of BBSes in the United States. Some are operated by corporations, but most are privately owned and operated. BBSes provide messaging services and file upload/download capabilities.

Bomb—The effect when rogue software activates. When a program reacts to certain conditions, this also is called a *logic bomb*.

Boot—The act of starting the computer.

Boot-sector infector—A virus that infects the startup code in the first sectors of a disk or diskette. Boot-sector viruses are more common than program-infecting viruses.

Bug—A programming error, often confused with a virus.

Callback—A high security modem feature that returns the caller's call at a preconfirmed number.

Chameleon—A program that simulates a legitimate program to gather information.

Checksum—An error correction scheme based on the total number of bits set in a file.

Command-processor infector—A virus that will infect COMMAND.COM.

CompuServe—International pay bulletin board service that contains hundreds of forums.

Cyberphobia—The fear of computers and the impact on our society.

Cyberpunk—A cracker or one who commits computer crime, often referred to as a subculture that praises cracking into computer systems.

Hacker—One who strives to master the computer.

LAN—Acronym for local area network.

Launch—To begin execution of a program.

Local Area Network—A network of computer equipment confined to a small area and interconnected by dedicated communications channels.

Logic bomb—A program or routine that activates on a certain logic or trigger.

Trojan Horse—A program that appears to be beneficial but in reality is tricking its way onto the hard disk for malicious purposes.

Virus—A program that self replicates by attaching itself to another program.

Virus scanner—A utility program that scans or searches for signs of a virus.

Worm—A program that replicates itself without attaching to or altering another program.

INDEX

E

F

Q-R